AN "OREL" HISTORY OF THE LEGENDARY PITCHER!

On how tough the major leagues really are:

"Most fans don't realize the incredible degree of ability required to reach the majors. The average fan would not be able to *catch*—let alone hit—a major league pitch.

"That's no put-down, it's a fact."

On what it feels like to pitch well:

"Only one in five times does it really simply flow out of my body with no adjustment. That's plain fun. But four of five times, it's just work, battling, looking for it, adjusting."

On how it feels up on the mound:

"I get a rush from being in sync, from knowing my mechanics are not only right but also unconscious. That's when it's the most fun. Rock and fire. Change speeds, change locations, trick 'em, fool 'em. Go for the strikeout only when you need it."

On how he felt right after the last World Series out:

"I was smiling, but I was still tight. I had not let go, not let it sink in. As I neared the dugout, I searched for Jamie in the stands. When I found her waving and cheering for me, I raised both fists and let it out. The grin came. Sharing it with her made the moment perfect."

Out of the Blue

OREL HERSHISER
WITH JERRY B. JENKINS

CHARTER BOOKS, NEW YORK

OUT OF THE BLUE

A Charter Book / published by arrangement with
Wolgemuth & Hyatt, Publishers, Inc.

PRINTING HISTORY
Wolgemuth & Hyatt edition / April 1989
Charter edition / April 1990

ISBN: 1-55773-341-4

Charter Books are published by The Berkley Publishing Group,
200 Madison Avenue, New York, New York 10016.
The name "CHARTER" and the "C" logo
are trademarks belonging to Charter Communications, Inc.

PRINTED IN THE UNITED STATES OF AMERICA

10 9 8 7 6 5 4 3 2 1

CONTENTS

To Jamie—
Nothing will ever mean
as much to me as you.

ACKNOWLEDGMENTS

Special thanks are due Mike Williams, Vicky Johnson, Ruth Ruiz, and their compatriots in the Dodger front office for help with photographs, clips, and statistics. Also to Tommy Lasorda for his time and input. Finally, to Jeanne Pearl and her associates for eleventh-hour tape transcribing.

FOREWORD

OF DREAMS AND ORDINARY PEOPLE

I thought a lot about who should write the foreword to my book. Who would lend it credibility? What well-known person might endorse it and enhance sales? I settled on me, but for neither of the above reasons. Because this is not a typical sports autobiography, I wanted to clarify a couple of things in advance.

First, I did not write this book for the money. In this country, a successful athlete with good counsel, firm priorities, and discipline does not need book royalties for financial security. I'm not saying I will turn down any proceeds from this book; I just want you to know that I have a larger purpose for the project than simply cashing in on a dream season.

Second, my image. I'm 6 feet 3 inches tall and weigh 190 pounds, a combination that has served me well. Admittedly, I have a funny name, in a baseball uniform I appear to have no chest, and my long arms and legs don't evidence my strength. Because of that, my reddish hair, and my toothy grin,

I've been described as Howdy Doody, less menacing than Mister Rogers, Opie from Mayberry, the batboy, a third tenor, a nerd, Ichabod, and paler than Greta Garbo. I told *Sports Illustrated*: "Let's face it, I'm just a pale guy with glasses, long arms, and a sunken chest. I look like I've never lifted a weight. I look like I work in a flour factory."

The question arises, of course, how all that jibes with the season I had in 1988:

- 23 wins during the regular season
- Breaking a pitching record no one—including me—thought would ever be approached
- Winning the National League Cy Young Award
- Being named Most Valuable Player in the National League Championship Series *and* the World Series, *The Sporting News'* Major League Player of the Year, *Sports Illustrated's* Sportsman of the Year, and the Associated Press Professional Athlete of the Year.

Some have written that no one is more surprised than I am. In a way, that's true. My wife, Jamie, and I have often said, "If that had happened to Dwight Gooden or Nolan Ryan, we'd be saying, 'Wow! What a fantastic year!'" but somehow, even though that fantastic year was mine, it still hasn't sunk in. I don't see myself as the best pitcher in the major leagues. I don't see myself as a superstar. I never want to become a prima donna. To be mentioned with Don Drysdale, Sandy Koufax, and Fernando Valenzuela is more than any pitcher should hope for.

But I have to be honest with you. While luck and

what I call the probabilities of baseball come into play periodically, there are concrete reasons why some teams and individual players are successful—even beyond their most outlandish fantasies.

A side of me resists admitting that I'm a good athlete. By admitting you're good at something, you put pressure on yourself. But no human dares to stand on a dirt hill 12 inches high with a 9-inch, 5-ounce sphere in his hand and face giants with clubs 60 feet, 6 inches away, unless deep inside he is confident of—even cocky about—his ability.

I always want to keep that cockiness deep inside and not allow myself to get bent out of shape by the unbelievable September and October I've just come through. No, I won't say it was all luck. But neither will I discount the impact on my success of my parents, my wife, my manager, my coaches, and my teammates.

And that brings me back to the purpose of this book. If it's not about cashing in and it's not a typical sports autobiography, what is it? What can you expect?

You'll learn that I was a late bloomer, not the typical superstar pro prospect from day one. I'm young enough to remember what it was like to want to be a big league baseball player. I haven't forgotten how mysterious the clubhouse, the locker room, and the dugout appear on the outside. My goal here has not been simply to describe what happened in games you probably saw on television or already read about. Make no mistake, there's a lot of pure baseball here, but I also wanted to reveal something new to you, something only I could tell you.

You see, I'm proof that great things can happen to

ordinary people if they work hard and never give up. You'll learn that it's not as easy as it looks. You'll know what it's like to be a big leaguer, a pitcher, a Dodger. You'll discover my sources of strength and faith.

Slip into my uniform. Be me for a couple of hundred pages. If it's as fun and exciting and rewarding for you as it has been for me, this book will have been a success.

Orel Leonard Hershiser IV
Pasadena, California

1

THE SERMON ON THE MOUND

My heart sank. The last person I wanted to see right then was Tommy Lasorda. What could he want? I wasn't sure I wanted to know. In fact, with a 2-2 record and a 6.20 earned run average, I was pretty sure I didn't.

But Ron Perranoski was the boss. When the pitching coach tells you the skipper wants to see you in his office, you don't stand around wondering what to do. "What does Tommy want, Perry?" I asked. I hoped against hope it didn't mean a trip back to the minor leagues.

"He'll let you know."

Uh-oh. "You goin' with me?"

"I'm invited, just like you. That's how Tommy works, you know. He wouldn't tell you anything without me there."

"Well, that's good. I guess. I hope."

It was early May, 1984, during my first full year in the big leagues. I was a Los Angeles Dodger relief pitcher, trying to hang on for dear life. I couldn't get anything going, couldn't maintain any consistency. I might get a guy or even two guys out, then I'd get too fine, too careful, and walk somebody. Tommy hated two-out walks. Almost as much as he hated two-out runs. And two-out runs too often followed my two-out walks.

I'd get even more careful, and before you knew it, someone had doubled up the alley. I'd be yanked, aired out for not doing what I was paid to do, and then I'd sit, wondering what was happening to my brief career.

As a rookie I was pretty much a non-entity with the Dodgers. I didn't have that casual relationship with the coaches that the veterans did. I wasn't consulted about strategy. Nobody cared what I thought was the right pitch in a specific situation. If I offered an opinion, it might just as likely be ignored as disputed. I was proving on the mound that I couldn't execute the pitches, even if I knew what they should be. Everyone said I had potential, the most frustrating label any player can have. I'd been hearing that since the day I signed.

Because I was young and looked younger, and because I was thin and wore glasses, and because I was known as a Christian athlete, I got the feeling people assumed I had no guts. Hershiser was too passive, too nice, too mellow to get the job done.

I was intimidated by Tommy Lasorda. Loud and brash and a real veteran baseball man, he was a manager any player would want behind him. He could be an encourager, but I didn't know where I stood. I feared I was on the bubble. There had to be guys in triple-A who could do better than I was doing.

And now he wanted to see me and my pitching coach. What could that mean? What could he want? Perry wasn't saying much. Did that mean he didn't know? Or worse, that he did know? Though the walk to Tommy's office seemed to take forever, I wished we hadn't arrived so soon. This was like being sent to the principal's office, but the stakes were much higher. I'd sure rather stay after school than be shipped back to Albuquerque.

Perry knocked, and Tommy waved us in. My mouth was dry, and I noticed Tommy wasn't smiling. He pointed to a couple of chairs, and Perry and I sat down. Tommy sat on the edge of his desk and looked down at me. I didn't take my eyes off him, and if I blinked I wasn't aware of it. I was prepared to agree with whatever he said, no matter what. I wondered if he could hear my heart.

"I invited you here with Ronnie because I never talk to a player without his individual coach present."

"Yes, sir, I know. I appreciate—"

He continued as if I hadn't said anything. "I wanted to talk to you about your game, the use of your ability, your mental approach to pitching."

I nodded.

"You remember how mad I was about how you pitched to Cruz the other day against Houston. . . ."

I nodded again. Did I ever. It was one of those two-out situations with two men on. Jose Cruz was a great contact hitter, a dangerous RBI (runs batted in) man.

". . . You throw low and away, ball one. Low and away, ball two. Low and away, ball three. He's takin' and you finally get a strike over, luckily, 'cause that one could'a been called low or outside, either one. He knows you can't afford to walk him, so he's sittin' on your three and one pitch, and what do you do?"

I didn't want to think about it, and I sure didn't want to talk about it. The worst thing was, Tommy was getting himself upset all over again just rehashing it. He grew louder. His face reddened. He leaned closer.

"You laid the ball in for him! Boom! Double and two runs! Hershiser, you're givin' these hitters too much credit! You're tellin' yourself, 'If I throw this ball over the plate, they're gonna hit it out.' That is a negative approach to pitching!"

I knew. I felt small and young and stupid. Sitting there nodding, I finally knew what he thought of me. My worst fears had been confirmed. I was hopeless. And, if it was possible, Tommy was getting louder. He was in my face now, those eyes bulging, his cheeks crimson. Sweat broke out on my forehead and the back of my neck. I didn't dare move even to wipe it off.

"You don't believe in yourself! You're scared to pitch in the big leagues! Who do you think these hitters are, Babe Ruth? Ruth's dead! You've got good stuff. If you didn't, I wouldn't have brought you up. Quit bein' so careful! Go after the hitter! Get ahead in the count! Don't be so fine with him and then find yourself forced to lay one in!"

As he sped on, louder and louder, something registered with me. Was that more than an airing out I just heard? Did a compliment slip by, disguised as a tongue lashing? I've got good stuff? He believes that?

Tommy continued, "If I could get a heart surgeon in here, I'd have him open my chest and take out my heart, open your chest and take out your heart, and then I'd have him give you my heart! You'd be in the Hall of Fame! If I had your stuff, I'd'a been in the Hall of Fame!

"I've seen guys come and go, son, and you've got it! You gotta go out there and do it on the mound! Take charge! Make 'em hit your best stuff! Be aggressive. Be a bulldog out there. That's gonna be your new name: Bulldog. You know, when we bring you in in the ninth to face Dale Murphy and he hears, 'Now pitching, Orel Hershiser,' man, he can't wait till you get there! But if he hears, 'Now pitching, *Bulldog* Hershiser,' he's thinkin', *Oh, no, who's that!?* Murphy's gonna be scared to death!"

We're nose to nose now, and I could use a towel on my face, but I don't even swallow, let alone move. "I want you, starting today, to believe you are the best pitcher in baseball. I want you to look at that hitter and say, 'There's no way you can ever hit me.' You gotta believe you are superior to the hitter and that you can get anybody out who walks up there. Quit givin' the hitter so much credit. You're better than these guys."

Part of me resented anyone thinking that I needed a nickname to make me tough and aggressive. No question I had not learned a proper approach to pitching. But I didn't think I needed a new name to make me stronger. Still, I couldn't get over that Tommy Lasorda felt I was worth this much time and effort. It hurt to hear him say what he said, but beneath it there had been a foundation of confidence in me. He believed I had more than potential. He believed I had big league stuff.

He was right that I had been treating big league hitters in a special way. I believed they had special ability. Which they did. What Tommy was telling me was that so did I. I wasn't some minor leaguer who had lucked his way up to the big club because it was a thin year for pitchers. I belonged on that mound just as much as the hitter belonged in the box.

Two days later against the San Francisco Giants the Dodgers needed a reliever in a difficult situation. The bullpen was full of tired, sore-armed pitchers, me included. The call came, "Can anybody down there pitch?"

I volunteered, despite a tender elbow and an arm weak from overwork. I strode to the mound reminding myself what a pleasant surprise it had been to learn that Tommy believed in me, thought I was special, needed me, thought I would be successful with an adjustment in my approach. I didn't know what I could do with my arm and elbow in the shape they were in, but my attitude was finally right.

From the dugout Tommy hollered, "C'mon, Bulldog! You can do it, Bulldog! You're my man, Bulldog!"

I challenged the hitters, kept the ball low, got ahead in the count on nearly every batter. In three innings, my arm feeling like a rag, I gave up only one run. Tommy's talk had worked. (He calls it his "Sermon on the Mound" and says he wishes he had taped it. "It'd sell a million, Bulldog!")

With my performance against San Francisco, I became a believer. I told myself that if I could do that when my arm felt terrible, think what I could do when I felt great. I still didn't like the nickname (I still don't), and I was still chagrined that anyone thought I needed it. But that day I became a big league pitcher. My attitude was revolutionized. I believed I deserved to be there, competing with big leaguers because I *was* a big leaguer. (The legendary Branch Rickey once said, "A big leaguer is a minor leaguer with a chance to play there.")

I learned years later that assigning a nickname to a player was Tommy's unofficial way of welcoming him to the big leagues. Until you showed him you could compete at that level, you were called by your given name. Franklin Stubbs was just Stubbs until Tommy decided he was worthy of a nickname. Then he became Cadillac. Mike Marshall was just Marshall until Tommy christened him Moose. Neither Tommy nor I knew then that he was right and that I could succeed at this level. But within two months, we had more to go on.

An injury to Jerry Reuss thrust me into a start on May 26. I joined the starting rotation for good June 29 against the Chicago Cubs, when I began the longest consecutive scoreless inning streak in the National League that year (33⅔ innings). I pitched four shutouts in July alone (and was named Pitcher of the Month), tied for the league lead in shutouts for the year, and finished third in ERA (earned run average), sixth in complete games, and eighth in strikeouts. I was third in Rookie of the Year voting.

My game had become focused. And the concentration motivated by the confidence Tommy instilled in me remains a key to my success today. Do you wonder how a pitcher could have had a 1988 like I had? Do you wonder how we Dodgers could have been motivated to maintain our intensity all through the season and the post-season, in spite of injuries and setbacks? We owe a lot of it to Tommy, of course, because he is a true motivator, encourager, cheerleader.

Knowing he believed in us allowed us to focus our energy, to eliminate distractions, to major on the fundamentals that outweigh everything, no matter what the task or pursuit. I benefited from realizing that there was too much to think about, too many variables, too many distractions if a pitcher tried to stay on top of every nuance of the game all the time. In my mind I narrowed my emphasis and priority to one thing and one thing only: the pitch.

PART TWO
THE PITCH

2

ATTITUDE

For a pitcher, with the game in its simplest form, it doesn't matter who's batting. It matters what the batter is doing. Is he pumped up? Is he a free swinger? That matters. That goes into the whole philosophy behind the pitch.

Once my catcher and I determine the pitch, that's all there is. There's nobody standing there then. I don't think about the next game, the next inning, the next hitter, the next play. There's only the next pitch. It's the only job I have.

There are certain gentlemen I don't wish to annoy by saying it doesn't matter who's batting. Names that come to mind immediately are Darryl Strawberry, Andres Galarraga, Tony Gwynn, Andy VanSlyke, Andre Dawson, Will Clark, Kevin McReynolds, and Barry Bonds. I hope several others will not be annoyed at my failing to mention them. But if I were a more dominant pitcher, if I had the fastball of a Dwight Gooden or a Nolan Ryan or a Roger Clemens, perhaps my attitude would be: "Here it comes." I confess I'd rather face a lineup of eighth

17

hitters and pitchers than front-line hitters any day, regardless of how competitive I am.

My stats might make it appear that I *am* a dominant pitcher, with my low ERA, my complete games, and my shutouts, but in truth I'm not the type who mows down hitters, striking out half of them. I was seventh in the National League in strikeouts in 1988, but that had as much to do with my leading the league in innings pitched as it did with my having overpowering stuff.

I'd be lying if I tried to say I don't have effective pitches. *Something's* working. All I'm saying is that it isn't the speed of my best fastball(around 90 mph) that makes me successful. I need every trick in my bag to keep hitters guessing, to keep them off balance. I'm not a junkballer by any standard, but I do take a decidedly mental approach to the game. I think, I study, I learn, I prepare, I work at it.

When I read what people say about me, I'm intrigued that they usually describe my mental approach and how tough a competitor I am—as opposed to my technical prowess—how good my sinker or curveball or changeup or fastball is. I don't read much about my being unhittable. Everything points to the mental.

For me, the reason is simple. Major league baseball, in spite of how fluid and easy we players tend to make it look, is a difficult and dangerous game. When they see such grace and poise in slow motion, most fans don't realize the incredible degree of ability required to reach the majors.

The average fan, unless he played at a fairly high level, would not be able to *catch*—let alone hit—a major league pitch. That's not a put-down; it's a fact.

Have you ever wondered how you might do against a Dwight Gooden? Consider this: not only would you likely not even foul off one of ten pitches, it's unlikely you would be able to force yourself to even stay in the batter's box when that long right arm came sweeping across his body. I get paid to face him, and the only reason I can stand in there is because of my confidence in his control.

If you've ever watched batting practice, you know there are portable fences and barriers all over the field—in front of the pitcher, at the sides and back of the plate, at each base. They protect the fielders from batted balls when they're taking grounders or throws from the outfield. Only a fool with his first field pass forgets that at every second he's hittable and makes sure he has a barrier between himself and the hitter. You even see major leaguers flinch, duck, or take a peek if they're surprised by the crack of the bat.

Baseball is a game, but there's nothing fun or funny about a big league fastball or a line drive screaming off the bat. That's why I narrow the game to priority number one: the pitch. And what goes into that pitch? Several things. When I talk pitching or teach pitching, I break the task into four major areas: attitude, mechanics, strategy, and regimen.

These all overlap, of course. The right attitude with the wrong mechanics results in failure. The right attitude and the right mechanics with the wrong strategy hunts the same result. Your attitude, your belief in yourself, your ability, and your mechanics—these allow you more strategy options.

Because this is not a typical sports book, I want to discuss those four areas one at a time before I cover what I think went into making me the type of competitor I am. Once you know my pitching philosophy and a little about me, then I'll take you into the locker room, into the dugout, and onto the field for the most amazing summer and fall I could ever hope to have.

When I take the mound to throw the first pitch, I expect to throw a perfect game. If I give up a walk, I intend it to be the only walk in the game. If I give up a hit, then my goal is throw a one-hitter. But I don't allow my mind to stray that far ahead. My one and only priority is the next pitch, not the no-hitter, the shutout, or even the out. If every pitch is thrown with the right mechanics and is rooted in sound strategy, and if my regimen has put me in proper physical and mental condition, the results will take care of themselves.

For instance, when I took the mound against the New York Mets for the '88 National League Championship series, I had pitched five straight shutouts, plus ten more scoreless innings in a no-decision. My ERA for September was 0.00. But could I think about shutting out the mighty Mets? The very thought was irrelevant. They had been shut out only four times in 160 games and had finished fifteen games ahead of the rest of the Eastern Division. They were second in the National League in batting average and first by a wide margin in runs scored—the only team to cross the plate 700 or more times.

It was crucial that I treat the Mets and the playoffs the way I treat every game. I had to narrow my focus, shutting out every distraction except the next pitch. That was manageable. Championships, victories, shutouts, no-hitters, perfect games—those are the results of 125 pitches thrown one at a time. The goal may be perfection, but the journey to success is made with eyes focused on the all-important next pitch.

Pitchers get into grooves that make them feel unbeatable. Such grooves can come from regimen and mechanics, but they can also come from pure coincidence. That's why you see big, strong rookies pitch three great games in a row, and then you never hear from them again. They fell upon the right mechanics, and their youth and strength carried them for a while. But such success can leave as quickly as it came.

I hate to admit that my 19-3 first full year as a starter in 1985 can in no way be compared to my 23-8 season in 1988. The difference is knowledge, knowing why the results are successful. I'm not saying there wasn't talent in 1985. But I hadn't channeled it, dissected it, and studied it. The talent was raw and much of the success was luck. Such success, as I proved the next year, is short-lived.

The only groove worth settling into is good mental discipline. Attitude. I now know what it takes to accomplish something on the mound. I can't know that I'm going to go out there and accomplish it every time, but I know the state of mind I need to be in. I know I can't allow myself to get too animated out there. I have to bear down, pitch for pitch. The key for me is to forget about results and concentrate on execution.

To maintain the right attitude during the season, I try to read very little about myself. If I've been successful, I might get a kick out of a rave review, but I put it behind me as quickly as possible. I strive to do my best, and I want to look good doing it, but concentrating on praise is a distraction that threatens the attitude I need. Complacency is death. Start thinking you've got it licked, and you're finished.

It's attitude that makes a pitcher willing to invest the time necessary to improve his mechanics and to learn and hone his strategy. Part of what motivates me is that I don't like being second best. I don't like believing that I can win, and feeling great confidence in my ability, only to go home after a loss knowing that I could have worked out harder or longer or more effectively.

I endured the agony of regret more than I care to remember, and I finally decided I wasn't going to have that excuse anymore. I told myself, "I'm in this to be a professional baseball player. This is my job. This is what I'm sinking my stakes into. I'm going to give it my best shot."

I need to make it clear that giving myself wholeheartedly to workouts was no guarantee of success in the win-loss column. It did, however, rule out laziness and bad work habits as excuses. No one likes to lose, but when I've done my best and my workouts have been good, I can look to strategy or mechanics or baseball probabilities when assessing what went wrong.

Sometimes nothing goes wrong, and you still lose. It's not unique for me to have my best stuff and be hit all over the yard. The Pittsburgh Pirates hit me last year like they owned me. In fact, if it hadn't been for them I might have won the ERA crown. I was a world beater against almost everybody else, but for them I was batting practice. Still, I didn't have to leave those games with my head hanging. I did my best, pitched as well as I knew how—and I was prepared.

Then there are those games when I look unhittable—maybe I pitch a 2- or 3-hit shutout with just a few runners reaching base—yet I'm miserable. My catcher and I know I left my best stuff in the bullpen, or maybe never had it. The fastball's not moving, the curve is flat, and the sinker doesn't. Yet because of great fielding plays, over-eagerness on the part of hitters, and the percentages going my way (like a half-dozen line drives hit right at somebody), I get credit for an impressive win.

I leave those games angry with myself, eager to get back to my workouts, ready to throw extra, to work on my mechanics. My coaches might tell me to back off a little, take it easy, because I'm in a groove. Yet I know otherwise.

The media might ask, "If that's how you pitch when you're off, what'll you be like when you're on?"

I might get shelled, that's what. There are no guarantees. And when that happens, I'll get a lot of unsolicited advice about working harder, working longer, and throwing more. Yet I may know that my stuff is just right and that I shouldn't tinker with anything. It's a strange game. I simply have to keep telling myself that a prepared pitcher is more likely to win than a lucky one.

I've told reporters after giving up 6 runs in three innings, "That's the best stuff I've had in a month and a half," and they look at me like I'm covering up. They're convinced I'm hurting, that I'm down, that I can't deal with the loss, that I can't admit I didn't have it. They think I'm telling them stories, probably because they're not used to pitchers admitting that their best stuff can be hit like that. There's always a temptation to believe that you can be hit only when you're having an off night. But what does that say about you and the competition? No one is as good as you are? No one else can get hot and be unbeatable in a given game? We've all played recreational sports with someone who will never give us our due when we win. It's as if he can't believe he lost and wants us to know that if he hadn't played so poorly, we wouldn't have won. It's insulting. And it's a bad attitude.

The perfectionist in me concentrates single-mindedly on every individual pitch. At this level of baseball you can destroy a perfect game, a no-hitter, a shutout, and even a victory with one mistake. One pitch that's not where you wanted to throw it, one pitch the hitter has guessed correctly, one pitch in an entire game that's a few miles an hour slower than it should have been or an inch higher or lower or more inside or outside than it should have been, and the pitcher pays.

Once you have performed at a certain level and you're past the point where it's luck, you know what's possible and you want to keep reaching that level every time. I have to deal with reality and the fact that I'm only human, just like any other athlete. But still I push to be the best Orel Hershiser I can be, and I never want to settle for less.

The fact is, only one in five times does it really simply flow out of my body with no adjustment. That's plain fun. But four of five times, it's just work, battling, looking for it, adjusting. I've got a good sinker one inning and it's gone the next. Good curve one inning, gone the next. It's maddening. It's frustrating. And every inning you walk to the mound, you start by finding out what's still working and what isn't. And nobody knows but you.

I don't like to fail, but I can handle it. That hasn't always been true, but as a Christian of ten years, I know where my strength comes from. I know that even if I give up a home run that makes me a goat, I'll survive. My wife and kids will still love me. God is still in His heaven. The world will not come to an end, regardless of my performance.

It's that same faith, though, that makes me determined to be a good steward of the mind and body I've been blessed with. If my faith merely made me accept defeat and failure, it would be a crutch—a weak, sad alibi. People who criticize Christians for being less competitive—and Christians who *are* less competitive—have missed the point of the faith.

It's my faith that lifts me up when I've failed. It's my faith that reminds me of my true insignificance when the world has been laid at my feet because of my success throwing a ball. To call myself a Christian and then not strive to be the best I can be and do the most I can with what has been given me would be the height of hypocrisy. Being a Christian is no excuse for mediocrity or passive acceptance of defeat. If anything, Christianity demands a higher standard, more devotion to the task.

Before I was a Christian, winning and losing were my only gauges for success. Now I know that diligence and execution are every bit as important. I can be satisfied and successful if I do what I know is right—preparing mentally and physically and using proper mechanics and strategy—even if I lose. But I also realize that I cannot take credit for a victory if probabilities have covered my shortcomings.

The bottom line on attitude for me is that I know I don't have enough talent to make up for mental mistakes at this level of baseball. I can't all of a sudden say, "I'm going to be Dwight Gooden," or "I'm going to be Nolan Ryan. I loaded the bases because of a lack of concentration, but now I'm going to simply wind up and blow my fastball past everybody and get out of this jam."

I don't have that kind of ability, and most pitchers don't. I have the ability to make accurate pitches with good movement at a variety of speeds, but I have to be in the game, on top mentally for every pitch. If I were still in the minors or in college, maybe I could overcome a mistake by turning up the heat. Maybe there wouldn't be enough talent on the other club to make me regret a pitch or two. But in the big leagues there's little margin for error. I was considered *the* major league pitcher for 1988, and I'm telling you, attitude is crucial. It begins and ends—and the pitcher succeeds or fails—with the all-important next pitch.

If you've made the big leagues, talent is assumed. But all the talent in the world and even a great attitude won't take you far if you don't really know how to pitch.

3

MECHANICS

The first thing a good pitcher needs is a thirst for knowledge. Any pitcher afraid to try something new for fear of failing will fail for lack of enough pitches to keep him in the big leagues. Every day a pro pitcher at some level is warned that if he does not come up with another wrinkle to expand his repertoire, he'll soon be shipped out.

Pitching is an art. Without a wide selection of pitches thrown properly for maximum effect, the artist is limited. One of the major elements in pitching strategy—as you will see—is surprise. If you have only two or three pitches and they always look the same, no hitter will be surprised. That's how dependent strategy is on mechanics. You can have mechanics with no strategy, but without mechanics, there is no strategy.

No organization I know of teaches pitching better than the Dodgers. More than just drumming into our heads how to pitch in certain situations and how to pitch to individual hitters, they teach us to dissect our own mechanics. We learn all that stuff. It doesn't just happen. If I'm erratic on the mound, I'll slow the game down and try to figure out what I'm doing wrong. I'll ask Perry if he detects anything. I'll ask Tommy. I'll ask my catchers, Sosh [Mike Scioscia] or Demper [Rich Dempsey]. I might even make a couple of throws to first just to give me time to think, to evaluate.

Fundamentally, mechanics have to do with the pitcher's body and his throwing motion. Whole books have been written about proper mechanics, but I can summarize the basics in a few words: Proper mechanics allow a pitcher to align his body in such a way that all his power and energy and speed and strength are concentrated in making his arm the perfect lever for delivering the ball to the plate. The legs are the foundation for setting up the lever. When the legs go, the arm usually follows. That's why you hear experts say that a pitcher's legs can be every bit as important as his throwing arm.

His balance, his foot placement, his pivot, his stride, his plant, his placement of fingers on the ball, the angle of his arm, the speed and degree of his body rotation, the speed of arm, and—maddeningly critical—his release point all go into the location, the velocity, and the movement of the pitch.

Pitchers who had been told they are naturals are sometimes afraid to evaluate all those complex elements for fear of messing up their minds. They know they can't concentrate on all that stuff every time they throw a pitch, so they rely on instinct and fire away. True, you can be reduced to a quivering mass if you try to run through a complete mental checklist as you make each pitch. But unless you examine and evaluate yourself in each area—one at a time—during workouts, how will you ever know what's going wrong when you lose your effectiveness?

When you're young and desperate either to reach the big leagues or stay there, this science of mechanics can be exasperating. You may spend endless hours in the bullpen working on your arm angle and release point, while in the meantime your stride has deserted you. Now you're opening up too much toward first base, and while you work on getting that back in line, your arm speed is off.

Complicating the whole picture is the fact that only certain mechanics remain constant with every pitch. If you're a veteran big leaguer and have a dozen or more variations of four or five pitches for you and your catcher to choose from, your mechanics have to become second nature or you'll spend the whole game trying to remember how to set yourself and move for each pitch. The goal is to be able to read the sign from the catcher and, if you agree with it, move automatically into the mechanics that will result in that precise pitch (with the proper movement) reaching the location you've chosen.

I have a sinking fastball* to either side of the plate, a cutter (which changes the direction of my fastball so it breaks instead of sinking) to either side of the plate, a curveball I throw at three speeds and three angles, a straight change—using the same arm speed and position as a fastball but with a grip and a release that slows it dramatically, and changeups to

---

*My sinking fastball should not be confused with a conventional sinker that may be thrown 20 mph slower. Many pitchers don't throw fastballs as hard as I throw my sinker.

different locations that I throw off my sinker and which look like batting practice fastballs. Different locations, different speeds, and slightly different arm angles on all those pitches give me a wide palette of choices. You can imagine how a minor mechanical problem with one variation of one pitch can affect an entire game. If it's true that every pitch is crucial, it's no wonder pitchers appear so deep in concentration all the time.

The three characteristics of any one pitch are *location*, *speed*, and *change of direction*. If you include how one pitch relates to another, you can add *change of speed* to that list. When I give pitching clinics, I like to ask kids which of those four is most important. The ones who love to throw hard say "Speed!" They've seen big leaguers strike out the side and heard the crowd and the broadcasters go crazy. The ones who have learned a few mechanics and have discovered they can throw a budding breaking ball will say, "Change of direction!"

The answer is location, and here's where mechanics moves toward strategy. Every hitter has a weakness. No one can get the sweet part of the bat to every part of the plate on one swing. The hitter has to guess, hope, anticipate, wager, give up to the pitcher a part of the plate.

Location is most important to me, then change of speed, then change of direction, then speed itself. I want to use location and change of speed to keep the hitter off stride, to mess up his timing to the point where he's hitting from his weakest point of power. If I get a hitter swinging, and my location or change of speed has fooled him, hopefully he'll have swung through his point of maximum power by the time he hits the ball, or he will not have reached that point yet. That way, even if he hits the pitch, it's not going out. It may be popped up, grounded, squibbed, anything but hammered.

Timing is so crucial to hitters that the goal of every pitcher is to show basically the same arm speed every time and have the ball come to the plate at the widest variety of speeds. The main way a hitter can judge the speed of the ball before it leaves the pitcher's hand is by the speed of the arm. The pitcher willing to invest the time in drilling himself on mechanics can develop the greatest illusion.

I also want the ball to come out at pretty much the same trajectory on every pitch. That way, the batter sees the same angle and the same arm speed and doesn't know until he really picks up a view of the ball that he may be getting one of ten or twelve pitches. He tries to make his job as simple as possible: see the ball and hit it. I try to make it as complicated for him as possible by fooling him. But once I've decided on the pitch and go to execute it, my job is simple too. I can throw only one pitch at a time.

The best pitches a pitcher can throw are those that move late, those upon which the hitter has registered and committed before they break. A curveball is hard to camouflage if it is released above the hand, as opposed to a fastball that comes straight from the hand and down to the catcher's glove. A bad curve comes out the top half of your hand and goes up before it comes down, which immediately says curveball to the hitter—at least to his subconscious. If I can throw a curve that looks like a fastball when it leaves my hand, the hitter will register fastball, prepare to hit a relatively straight pitch, and—I hope—see it explode away from him at the last instant.

That kind of a curve is almost impossible to hit. Even if he knows it's coming, if it breaks late it's most successful. My curveball is at its best not when it's breaking the most or the sharpest; it's at its best when it looks most like my fastball.

I like to work backwards. Rather than work on my arm and see what it can produce, I try to determine what a pitch did, how the ball moved, and whether it achieved what I wanted. Then I try to work that back into my arm, its angle, its speed, and the release point. It has been gratifying for me to see the improvement of my pitches over the last few years. Just two seasons ago scouts and other experts rated my fastball, curveball, and sinker as exceptional but not among the best in the league. They rated my changeup as good but not exceptional.

After last season, Ron Perranoski said Clem Labine was the only other pitcher he'd "seen in thirty years with a similar combination of the hard running sinker and deadly overhand curveball." Of course Ron, along with Sandy Koufax and Dave Wallace, had a lot to do with teaching me the mechanics that improved my pitching. *Baseball Digest* said I was the best breaking ball pitcher in the National League last year. I say that not to brag but to raise a torch for the importance of mechanics.

Peter Gammons, baseball writer for *Sports Illustrated*, says, "Few pitchers can claim *two* pitches that are among the very best in the game, but Hershiser can with his sinker and curveball."

Tommy Lasorda, who's seen a lot of great pitching

in his day, believes my changeup is my most improved pitch, but also says this: "Bulldog's got a fastball that moves. That's the important thing. As a manager, I'd rather see a pitch move half the size of the baseball than see one thrown 95 miles an hour straight as a string. In the big leagues, you could stand on the mound with a pistol and shoot bullets at the hitters, and eventually they'll time 'em. The most effective thing you can have is movement on the ball."

When a big league pitcher is on, when his mechanics are sound and everything is working right, eight times out of ten his catcher should be able to catch the ball while hardly moving the glove. A catcher who truly receives the ball, gathering it in in a fluid motion, can actually expand the strike zone for his pitcher. If he's forced to dart and stab at the ball with his glove, a close pitch will look worse to an umpire. A pitch even a couple of inches off the corner may be called a strike if the catcher hardly has to move. And when you get into balls and strikes, you're talking strategy.

4

STRATEGY

Thanks to the dominant pitching of the 1960s and particularly the abilities of three pitchers who were stellar in 1968, strategy is even more important to the man on the mound now than it was then. After that incredible year, during which Bob Gibson of the St. Louis Cardinals accomplished a *season-long* ERA of just 1.12 (including 47 consecutive scoreless innings), Denny McLain of the Detroit Tigers won 31 games, and Don Drysdale of the Dodgers pitched a record 58⅔ consecutive scoreless innings, baseball's powers-that-be responded.

The height of the mound was reduced from 18 to 12 inches, and the strike zone was shrunk as well. I pity American League pitchers who have to face designated hitters and don't even have the luxury of facing each other every three innings. The designated hitter rule virtually eliminates automatic outs. Nowadays, we big league pitchers have to create every legal advantage we can.

I know many also create illegal advantages by scuffing or cutting or adding substances to the ball, but I don't. I've been accused of throwing a spitter because my sinker moves so much, but I take that as a compliment. I have a pretty credible witness for my plea of innocence. Whitey Herzog has said: "A spitter? Hershiser doesn't throw a spitter! How do I know? I've seen his pitches sink during warmups. Who cheats when you're warming up? Who loads up in the bullpen?"

So, for those of us with only the legal elements to be juggled and selected from, pitching may sound more scientific and computer-like than it is. Yes, it can be complex, and, yes, I study videos and film and make notes on the opposition. But when I'm on the mound, I'm as likely to go against conventional wisdom as with it. I'm as likely to defy the percentages as follow them, for the sake of surprise.

I love to be creative on the mound. I love to get into a rhythm with my catcher, to get to the place where we both know which pitch should be next, to be able to get him to change without even shaking him off. Sometimes I don't want the hitter to know I'm shaking off a sign, so I just continue to stare until I get the sign I want. If I'm out there shaking off signs, the hitter knows we're flustered and that he's not likely to get the pitch I would usually throw in that situation.

At times it's good to shake off a sign just to confuse the hitter. If Sosh and I have been thinking alike all night and the sequences have begun to show some logic and predictability, I may shake off the very sign I wanted and just wait until he gets around to that one again before I nod. Then the batter—I hope—has no idea what's going on.

I get a rush from being in sync, from knowing my

stuff is good and is working, from knowing my mechanics are not only right but also unconscious. That's when it's the most fun. Rock and fire. Change speeds, change locations, trick 'em, fool 'em, work 'em. Go for the strikeout only when you need it. Otherwise, get out of there with as few pitches as possible.

The perfect inning? Three straight pitches that result in popouts or groundouts. Can't beat that. Great for the arm. Great for the confidence. Great for the team.

Rather than seeing all the elements like input for a computer, I would rather think of them as paints to be mixed. Green might be called for, but mix it with yellow and no one will ever expect it. Add some hues, change some tone, add a splash of this and a dash of that. Conventional wisdom says never throw a changeup to a weak hitter. He'll sit back on it, be thrilled to see it, tee off on it. So I might go almost a whole game, the first three times I face a hitter, and work him hard with my best stuff, my heaviest fastball, the sinker with the most movement. Then, in the last inning, if the game isn't on the line, I may throw him three straight changeups. If I'm successful, the first one will stun him. He'll think he's being set up for the fastball. The second one will confuse him. No way in the world he'll expect the third. The key is to bury the bad hitters because the good hitters are going to eventually get their hits regardless. Bear down on numbers seven, eight, and nine, because three, four, and five will be up soon enough.

When I have my best stuff, I'd rather face the contact hitters than the power hitters. If my sinker is working, I want the singles hitters to make contact, because the ball isn't going anywhere anyway. But the big guys, the free swingers, can kill you with one swing, even if you've got a great curveball or sinker working.

If I'm facing a key hitter, a third or fourth man early in the game with none on and two out, I might pitch right at his strength. The scouting report may warn against an inside fastball. I may throw one anyway, to test whether mine's really working that day. And even if he hits a double, until I need to show him my best stuff in a tight, late situation, he may never see it. Let him get used to off-speed stuff, or pitches he likes. Let him hope to see more of that later, then I can move to my best stuff when I really need it.

There are risks you take early that you wouldn't take late in a close game. Pitch selection depends entirely on the situation and the stage of the game. If the big hitter drives one out on me, that's what he gets paid for, and I learned a lesson. That one run shouldn't beat me, because my team should be able to score, too. In the eighth, I hope that same hitter has no idea what I might throw.

Every time I throw a pitch to a veteran player, it's a cat and mouse game. If the hitter is a rookie or a young player, he may be too intimidated to try to outguess me. He's just hoping to make contact, and that makes him dangerous. I don't know his strengths and weaknesses beyond what I can tell from the few times we may have scouted him.

But the veterans have faced me before. I know them; they know me. I have to remember my sequence of pitches. Did I set this hitter up last time with two curveballs in the dirt and then jam him with an inside cutter? Did I simply go after him with my best sinker? If it worked last time, it may not work this time. But is he thinking the same? Is he sure I won't come back with the same combination two at bats in a row? Two games in a row?

At a certain level, with experienced, crafty hitters and pitchers, the game can be more mental than physical. Imagine what veteran hitters must process when they face a starter who's been in the league as long as they have! It's great fun to watch, and I've been around only five years.

Another way to go after a hitter is to be obvious. Set him up conventionally so he virtually knows you're coming in with the curve. He's ready for it, eager to hit it, and you throw it. His eyes are wide, and as he steps and opens the hips and commits, he realizes that though it's the curve he knew was coming, it's not the speed he thought, or it's not in the location he wants. Too bad. Too late.

If I'm throwing to a righthander who is often fooled by a sweeping curve, I'll throw one that looks like it may break over the plate but which actually sails away from him. With a lefthander who has a sweet spot low and inside, I may throw the curve that looks like it's going there but which breaks harder and farther. If I do throw a pitch low and in to him, I want it to look like it's in his sweet spot before it buries itself below his knee where he can't reach it.

How much can a big leaguer make a ball break? Some people say a few inches to half a foot. But anyone doing it for a living can tell you that if you throw one right, a big, slow curve can appear to break from the batter's shoulder all the way to the dirt, three or four feet. The problem with that pitch is that it can split the plate and still be hard to get called a strike. It starts high and finishes with the catcher on his knees, and it just doesn't look like a strike unless the batter swings at it. It's a low-percentage proposition. It is easier to get a short, harder, breaking-ball called for a strike.

How far off the plate can you be and still get a called strike? Let me put it this way. I believe that in the big leagues the outside corner is definitely bigger than the inside corner. The outside of the plate is the pitcher's and the inside is the hitter's. That's partly for the protection of the hitter. If we were getting strikes called on pitches very far inside, there'd be more pitches thrown there and more batters hit. You need half the ball to hit the inside corner to get a called strike, but on the outside corner you can occasionally get a call when you're actually slightly off the corner. I've had games where I've pitched consistently off the outside corner all night and I get that strike call because I'm making my pitches and hitting the target my catcher is setting. A pitch off the corner can be a strike if you are making your pitches, hitting your target.

I know that sounds like heresy to the purist, but things eventually even out. If Sosh or Demper have been setting up low and outside all night and I've been right on the money there, then I slip and fire one that splits the plate, the batter freezes and takes it, and I'm just as likely to get a ball called.

I never argue with an umpire during the inning, but while walking off I may say, "Where was that pitch?" and the umpire will say, "Right down the middle, but it was not where you wanted it."

I never try to show up an umpire. I don't see any future in it. That's all part of pitching strategy, too. They have a job to do, and it doesn't do me any good to try to make them look bad, even if they do make a mistake. I make mistakes too, but I wouldn't want an umpire glaring at me because of it.

Sometimes I'll just look in and study the plate after a call I think was wrong. Veteran umpire Bruce Froemming once told me, "You know, you're great, Hershiser. You don't moan or argue, but you're quite a surveyor out there."

Pitchers and umpires gain respect for each other over the years. You learn about each other. Just like I get in rhythm with my catcher, I can find a rhythm with an umpire occasionally. If I wear out a spot with consistently fine pitches, I know where his strike zone is that night. If I'm sporadic, I haven't helped him settled in, and I get fewer calls going my way.

That's what makes pitching so much fun. I stand on that mound facing a catcher who is all for me, a hitter who is totally against me, and an umpire paid to be impartial. I want to be in sync with my catcher, gain the respect of the umpire, and keep the hitter off balance.

The only thing I don't like about my job is that I can't do it every day. I hate waiting. I hate being out of the action. But the human arm was not designed to throw objects overhand. Pitchers need three to four days to recuperate. Underhand softball pitchers, even the fastballers with the windmill whip motions, can pitch several games a day, several days in a row. But when a grown man trains his body to hurl a sphere 90 mph overhand, he's breaking down small tissue fibers and causing swelling.

That's why we ice our arms for fifteen to twenty minutes after every game. That's why I use a climbing machine on off days to get the blood flowing through that arm and to flush the junk out of my system. And those are the first two arm-preserving steps in a regimen that will determine whether I can pitch a full career.

5

REGIMEN

With a sport as demanding as baseball, a professional owes it to himself to be in top physical condition all the time. The intensity at that level is so fierce that only a primed competitor can hope to succeed. Occasionally you hear of someone with so much natural ability that he can hit near .300 with very little batting practice, or of someone who can win 15–18 games a year despite poor work habits. Those are rare exceptions. That type of player may impress fans and sports writers, but he is not respected by his peers. His colleagues can only wonder how great he might have been if he had really applied himself.

When you're of average size and strength and ability and your future depends on your performance, you work hard out of a sense of fear and desperation to stay in the game. Once you have reached some level of achievement and respect, the fear may be gone, the desperation to hang on may be less, but the importance of maintaining your edge is just as urgent. How else can you hope to compete with the strong, young bodies entering the league every year or with the veterans who have found new and better ways to condition themselves? Even if you can keep track of all the players-in-waiting on your own club, without a plan you can't maintain any advantage against the competition—players you either have to face or worry about being traded for.

My regimen includes more than just working out, staying in shape, and laboring at mechanics. Everything that has to do with getting me in the right frame of mind, I consider vital. That means everything from avoiding distractions the day before a start, to the way I eat, the amount of sleep I get, how I act and want to be treated at home, when I leave for the stadium, and how I put on my uniform— everything.

I'll be frank with you. I love every detail of it. From the first rumble of awareness in my mind that I'm within one game or one day or my next start, all the way through to the point where I finish my warm-up tosses and the first hitter steps in. That whole routine involves drudgery and hard work, but it also provides ceremony and framework and measurable steps that allow me to evaluate my performance. If I have a bad outing, I can look back to a distraction, something that happened at home, a rushed workout, a lack of concentration, the wrong food, something.

I get bored easily so I like to be creative and vary my approach, but some elements of my regimen are inviolable. I may chase down flyballs at top speed during a half hour of batting practice rather than put myself through a set of boring wind sprints, but I would never change from my pasta-based, high carbohydrate pre-game meal. To eat red meat or something greasy that would stay on my stomach until game time would be crazy, not creative. I always get in my climbing and weight training, too.

It might surprise you to know how important my wife is in my training regimen. Jamie is crucial to how well I do on the field, from simply keeping the house in order and making sure we're not in a tense moment at home, to making sure things run smoothly, to making sure people don't get at me on game day. She doesn't bring me any decisions, even related to the business or the kids—except for emergencies, of course—the day before or the day I pitch. On those days she answers the phone and protects me from everything and everyone.

I'm getting into my "zone," my game mode. I don't want a crisis or a decision or a phone call that interrupts my train of thought. I may not be thinking only about the game, but I don't need pressure. For those two days, no matter what it is, Jamie takes care of it. It's all on her shoulders. She knows that even though I'm there, she can't bother me.

That may sound harsh or even demeaning, and I never want to treat her like a servant. But unless it's life or death, Jamie takes care of it, and I consider that a tremendous gift of love. I never want to take her for granted. I know her job is not easy, and I appreciate her more than I can ever express.

It has be be tough on Jamie's ego and self-esteem to be married to a major league baseball player, a local star, and now a World Series MVP. Her identity is "wife of . . .," and that would be hard for anyone. So many things revolve around me. People who call want a piece of me, want to talk to me. The phone means instant attention. Once people get me on the phone, I'm theirs. Sometimes, we just have to turn it off.

The difference between the number of calls we got when I was just a local personality and the number we get now after the World Series is incredible. It must wear on Jamie every time my attention is diverted from her to whoever is calling. I'm whatever they want and need me to be, but she often gets treated like a second-class citizen. Often people won't even give her a message for me, like she's chopped liver, as if she is not as important in the business and decision-making end of things as I am. She makes as many decisions as I do, and she can even say no for me. Yet people act as if her word doesn't mean anything. They think, *If I can get to Orel, I know I can convince him my cause is good.*

But I don't overrule her, and people will eventually learn that. My relationship with her is the root of my success on a human level. If I'm not happy at home, I can't perform on the field. I can't be as intense. I can't have a good, solid workout. I'm not mentally strong enough to do that. I've tried. I've gone to the park on days when we've had disagreements or when things are tense at home, and I'm not the same person. I can't concentrate on the game as much or train as hard. I know how important it is to have a positive, solid marriage.

I look like a strong, together person, and that makes it hard for Jamie to believe how important she and the boys are to my equilibrium. That's not something natural to say every day, but it's true.

Wives can also destroy careers. When you're going through a tough time, if your wife isn't supporting you, you start to believe it's time to quit. If you have five bad outings, you need to come up with a new pitch, the parent club looks down on you, you assume you're about to get released, and you don't know what to do. Meanwhile, if your wife agrees with all your doubts, you're finished. If you get reinforcement for your negative vibes, your performance will suffer even more.

But if your wife says things like, "it'll be okay," "let's pray about it," "we can take care of this," "you'll work through it," and "it was just a rough outing," and she's there with support and love, then you can put it behind you and move on.

The toughest time for Jamie is when I begin to get on my "game face." The game face is the one you see on television or in pictures of me when I have zeroed in on the target, I'm totally immersed in the game, and nothing can distract me. Over the years I have discovered that I must find that serious, all-business, aggressive, almost mean side of my personality that allows me to compete at the big league level.

That person is so intense he won't let one detail slip by and will bear down on every pitch. I can't be the happy-go-lucky, down-to-earth Orel when I go out to face the opposition. I have to be tough, and that means looking deep within for my alter ego.

The biggest struggle I have is postponing that zoning, because though it is crucial for my success, if it comes on too early I can peak too soon. While Jamie is protecting me from distractions, she is also careful to watch for signs that I'm zoning everything else out too soon. Jamie is my mirror.

"Don't get it on yet," she'll remind me the day before a start. "Please, it's too early."

Sometimes that aggravates me and I tell her to let me be myself, that I have to be this way to compete effectively. But more often I realize she's right. I have to interact with her and the boys, and though it's good to be protected, I don't want to get too far into the alternate personality too early.

During the game before the one they are to pitch, Dodger starters are allowed to leave after the second inning. We are to go home, have a good meal, get a good night's rest, and be ready the next day. If I haven't seen the team I'm going to face, I might stay around a few more innings to see who's hot, watching either from the dugout or the TV room. Then I head home to a good meal and an early bedtime. I may listen to the game on the radio, but I do not allow myself to get too excited one way or the other. If I do, I tend to get pumped up too early about my own game. When the adrenalin starts flowing, I find it impossible to fall asleep.

What works best for me is a pleasant distraction, whether it be Jamie or Quinton or even baby Jordan. There's a fine line between being able to think about my game without starting to get wired, zoned, steely, quiet, intense. The game face is necessary, but for my sake and the sake of my family, I put it off as long as I can. That benefits my game, too, because the game face that evidences I'm zoned is a drain on my system. It's vital in a game. Too early, it's debilitating.

On game day, I do what my body tells me. If it wants to get up at nine, I get up. If it wants to stay in bed till noon, I stay in bed. If it wants pancakes for breakfast or a milkshake at noon, I go with the flow. At 2:30, however, it's time for another high carbohydrate pasta meal that will be well-digested by game time and will give me energy.

Early in my career I was a big beef man, lots of hamburgers and steaks, red meat at least twice a day. Now I might eat red meat twice a month. You live and learn. The last thing I want in my system is something that will make me feel blah by game time and weigh me down, making me feel like I don't even want to be there.

Between my meal and game time I need time alone, to think and pray and listen to music and read my Bible. In no way do I do this as if God will smile upon me for being faithful or diligent. He's more than a friend I talk to when I need to relax and think about something other than baseball.

When it's time to leave for the ballpark, I still try to maintain some equilibrium. For big games, during the scoreless inning streak, the playoffs, and the Series, I let the stereo blast, keeping my mind off the game as long as possible. I may not even chat with the guard at the gate but simply smile and wave as I pull through.

By the time I get out of the car and start heading toward the locker room, I have truly become a multiple personality or at least schizophrenic. I don't mean to make light of a psychological problem, but I become deeply aware that I am two distinct personalities. There's the typical Orel who will greet friends and fans and be light and happy and normal. At the same time, beginning to exist deep inside me is the other Orel Hershiser. That Orel has the ability to narrow his concentration to the regimen of game preparation. He can become aggressive, stubborn, focused, intense. He will miss no detail. He will even push his teammates to keep their heads in the game when necessary. When I'm the starting pitcher, that Orel might chastise a teammate who's not concentrating, not serious. That would seem totally out of place for the other Orel. But for this Orel, the pitch, the next pitch, is all there is to him. Everything he does from that point will center around that.

It's time to dress for baseball.

6

GAME DAY

For some reason, even when I'm wearing tie shoes I usually just kick them off from the heel and loft them into my locker. While I'm sitting there in my underwear it's not unusual for someone like first baseman Franklin Stubbs to stroll by. I call him by his nickname.

"Hey, Cadillac," I'll say.

"How ya' doin', O? Listen, can I get you to sign this for a friend?"

He hands me a hat, and I sign it under the bill with a "best wishes" and the name of his friend. Before I'm dressed I might trade autographs a couple of dozen times with teammates. There's always a ball or a pennant or a hat or just a piece of paper someone wants signed. It's part of all of our jobs.

While I'm small-talking with the guys, I'm churning inside. I'm thinking about the team I'll face tonight, remembering what happened against them last time, good and bad. I have a bedrock confidence in my regimen and mechanics. I'm still mulling over strategy; that will solidify as I look at the latest scouting reports, talk to the coaches, and see what pitches are working.

The first article of clothing I put on is a pair of long-legged underwear that reaches to just above the knees. Then comes a jockstrap. Before the game I will put a cup between the underwear and jockstrap, not in a strap with an insert for the cup. I find the cup is less a nuisance that way, moving with me and not getting in the way. Very few major leaguers at any position play without a cup. On the rare occasion when I find myself on the mound without one, I make a quick trip to the clubhouse between innings. If I throw a 90 mph fastball to a line-drive hitter and don't get the glove down in time, I will indeed wind up the third tenor I supposedly look like.

For now, the cup stays in the locker, and I pull on a long-sleeved sweat shirt. No sense getting cold in the locker room. Next I pull on two pairs of sanitary stockings, then my stirrups and an elastic band about two inches thick that goes around my calf just below the knee to hold the stockings and stirrups in place. The sanitaries and stirrups actually reach several inches above the knee, so I then fold them down over the elastic and back up to make a smooth gathering for the uniform pant to cover.

Next comes the uniform shirt and pants. The current style is to have the pant extend almost all the way down the leg so that only a few inches of the stirrups show. In fact, some players have sanitaries with the stirrups painted on. From the stands it's impossible to tell that they aren't really wearing stirrups.

After my belt and warm jacket are on, I head out,

leaving my hat in my locker. On the way to the field I grab two or three bats, my batting helmet, and my batting gloves. I leave everything I need for the game—except for what I'll use in batting practice—in the bat rack. That way I don't have to worry about anything except my zone, my game face, my mental preparation when I come in from the bullpen.

With one bat, my helmet, and my batting gloves I head to the batting cage and am generally the first hitter in the first group of four or five, made up of the starting pitcher, the nonstarters, and the pinch hitters. Pitchers take batting practice every day at home, while on the road they take it only on the day they're pitching.

The first hitter serves as captain of his group, calling out how many swings everyone will take each time up, and then how many swings each gets when we have just a minute left. That's the lightning round when you see players running into the cage to hit one pitch and then get out quickly in hopes of getting another turn.

On days when I'm pitching, I start by bunting, then move into the fake-bunt-and-swing play, then get in my regular swings. Because of the energy it takes to jump in and out of the cage and worry about getting in a few more swings, I pass up the lightning round and let the other guys have the remaining time. I dump my helmet and gloves and bat in the bat rack so that's taken care of for the night, then I head back to my locker to shed my jacket, jersey, sweat shirt, and underwear. I change into a dry tee shirt and gym shorts before going to the TV room to relax, see what's on, and take a look at the scouting report. I leave the sanitaries and stirrups in place.

We might watch game shows to let our minds idle, or we might try to find the Mets or Braves games already begun in the East. Soon batting practice is over and the troops start filing in. Some will slap me on the back and offer encouragement. Others will engage me in small talk to keep me loose. I don't need it, but I appreciate it.

Early in my career I didn't like to talk before a game, and until players get to know the various wishes of the starters, they pretty much leave them alone. It's a don't-speak-to-the-starting-pitcher-unless-he-speaks-to-you rule. Everybody knows I'm open to conversation now. My zoning operation is going on full tilt inside.

If the game is the first in a series, we'll have a team meeting where we go over the scouting report and discuss every hitter. Billy DeLury, our traveling secretary, might have some instructions about arrangements for the next road trip and ask for names of wives or other family members who have to be approved for the charter flight.

Tommy Lasorda will frequently deliver an informational pep talk, and then it's time for me to get my rubdown and start really getting ready. If the meeting runs a little long, I may have to leave early so I don't get behind schedule. It won't be long before Perry starts looking for me in the locker room so we can head down to the bullpen.

Assistant trainer Charlie Strasser, whom I've known since my minor league days, gives me a ten-minute rubdown, then physical therapist Pat Screnar takes another ten minutes to stretch my arm and rotator cuff area. He also works my elbow. After some arm stretching exercises I go back into the locker room and dress completely for the game with a cup, a fresh long-sleeved blue undershirt and jersey, and my uniform pants. Finally I'm ready for a vigorous session with trainer Bill Buhler, who stretches the rest of my body.

I'm not superstitious, but I will rarely deviate from that schedule. I want everything to go like clockwork so that when I first see Perry, and it's almost time to warm up, I'm ready to completely zone myself, inside and out, and set my focus on the game, the opposition, the mechanics, the strategy . . . the pitch.

For a 7:35 P.M. home game, I want to be on the front edge of a practice mound with a ball in hand so I can take my first warm-up toss at exactly 7:15. For the first ten minutes I throw just fastballs to Beach [bullpen coach Mark Cresse]. I'm on flat ground and not throwing hard yet, but I'm throwing with a purpose. My eyes are glued to his glove and my game face is on. I don't even look like the same guy who pulled out of the driveway just hours before.

I'm thinking about the position of my body, getting my hip in line, releasing the ball at a precise spot every time. I work on my stride, on the mechanics for my sinker, on getting my fingers inside. When my arm starts to feel loose, I back Mark up, sometimes right out of the bullpen gate and onto the field. Now I'm playing long toss, airing out my arm with throws of close to a 100 feet.

As we get closer to game time, Mark crouches behind a plate and I step up on a bullpen mound. Now I'm throwing in earnest. I want to see what I've got. What will be working tonight? What selections will I be able to make from my repertoire?

At game time the man behind the plate is usually Mike Scioscia (sometimes Rick Dempsey). By now I want to have a feeling of confidence in every aspect of my game. I want the mechanics and execution to be automatic so I can concentrate on strategy, on art, on creativity. I want it to flow, to be rhythmic. I want Sosh to start knowing what's happening with me. I want to throw with a purpose and think of nothing but the next pitch. As I've said, for a pitcher, with the game in its simplest form, it doesn't matter who's batting. Once I determine the pitch, that's all there is. It's the only job I have.

PART THREE

THE PITCHER

7

"LITTLE O"

To know what makes me tick today, you have to know a little about where I came from. Since I can't imagine that anyone would care about the life story of a 30-year-old baseball pitcher, I'm going to highlight certain memories that may shed some light on who I am now.

And who am I now? The statistics are in the appendix and the story of the season is in parts four and five, but even I have to wonder what makes me so competitive. What makes Mike Marshall say I'm the most competitive person he's ever known? Why do I love to win at everything, including cards and table games, golf, pool, you name it?

What makes me befuddle the doctors? You didn't hear about that? Listen to this one. It's unbelievable.

It starts one week before spring training last season, yeah, 1988, the miracle year. People who saw me collapse on the Los Angeles North Country Club golf course that day in early February would never have predicted I would even have a successful season, let alone one for the books.

And it wasn't my knee acting up either. I had had arthroscopic surgery at the end of the previous season after suffering most of the year. I'm not blaming my 16–16 record on that; in fact, I never even griped about it, never told anyone. I considered it a nagging type injury that everybody plays with, and there's nothing worse than a bunch of players sitting around crying about all their aches and pains.

Torn cartilage had made it difficult for me to plant my foot, so I had to have something done. Arthroscopy is that surgery where they don't have to slice you open but do all the work through tiny incisions. I knew it was the best thing for me, but my leg was so stiff and sore for weeks after that that I feared my career was ruined. I'm the type who likes to get right back into the swing of things and start running, climbing, lifting, and throwing. My knee was so sore, I worried I might never do any of that again.

But eventually the knee cleared up and was stronger than ever, so that wasn't the problem on the golf course four months later.

I was out there with Lowell Graham, a good friend, and John Werhas, a former Dodger and now our baseball chapel leader—a man who means a lot to me and has helped me grow in my faith. We were having fun.

We enjoyed a sandwich at the turn, but on the back nine I felt a burning sensation in my stomach. I thought maybe it was food poisoning. I would hit a shot, then move to the edge of the fairway and lean against a tree, hoping I would be sick and be done with it. But it kept getting worse. Of course, it didn't interrupt the game.

The more breaks I took, the more John and Lowell

were concerned, but I downplayed it, assuring them it was just gastritis or a sour stomach or something I ate. I coughed up a little acid occasionally, but I got no better.

I bent over a shot on the eighteenth hole and a sudden pain, low in my gut, drove me to my knees. My partners grabbed for me, but after a few seconds I was able to stand. And, naturally, I finished my round. I decided I was hungry. We'd had only a bite at the turn, so I was sure a decent lunch at the buffet table in the clubhouse would cure me.

As we stood in line, waiting to get at the food, suddenly nothing looked appetizing. The pain made me light-headed and I certainly didn't want to embarrass myself. When a trip to the bathroom didn't make me feel better, I told the guys I needed to go home. They were worried, but I assured them I could make it. I needed some rest. Maybe I was coming down with something.

I tried to drive all the way from the west side of Los Angeles to my home in Pasadena, but I had to stop several times and open the door, hoping to lose enough from my aching stomach to provide some relief. I was sweating, dizzy, and short of breath. I drove like a madman to get home before I passed out.

When I got home, Jamie was out and Mabel, our live-in friend and helper—who is always there for us—looked alarmed when I staggered in. "I'm okay," I told her. "I need a shower and a nap." I went straight upstairs, eager to lie down. As soon as I got to the bathroom I vomited gastric juices and suffered dry heaves that made me wish I were dead. I hoped that by emptying my stomach, I would feel better, the way it usually works. I'd never been this sick.

When Jamie got home she found me unconscious on the bathroom floor and helped me into bed. Nothing made me feel better. Finally she called Dr. Mickey Mellman, one of our team physicians, and described my symptoms: chills, pain, vomiting, dry heaves, and no relief. "Get him to the hospital," he told her.

My brother Gordie was staying with us, so he helped Jamie get me into the car and drive me to the hospital. Every few minutes I moaned aloud with the pain. I was ashen-faced and too sick even to worry about what could be wrong. Gordie got me situated in a chair in the reception area and went to the desk to sign me in.

"He'll have to come over and sign in himself," a nurse told him.

In spite of seeing his brother half dead, Gordie retained his sense of humor. "Sure, I'll bring him over, if you want him to throw up all over you." She let him handle the paperwork.

I was put on a gurney and rolled into an emergency room. With a sheet up to my neck, my breathing shallow, dry heaving, and moaning, I was a sight and a curiosity. It got around that the noisy near-corpse on the cot was a Dodger pitcher. "Oh, I know you," someone would say.

I couldn't even look at them. "Oooooh!" I would reply.

Even the doctor was impressed. "I saw you pitch," he said. A rush of stomach fluid got him back to business.

I was switched to a hospital where Dr. Mellman

could look after me. Finally, after ultrasound, lower GI, and other procedures you don't care to read about any more than I care to write about them, I was prepped for an emergency appendectomy. It was a relief just to know what was wrong.

Dr. Jeff Hyde performed the operation and removed my appendix before it ruptured. Otherwise, I would have been down for weeks. The operation was almost miraculous. I had the advantage of being in top physical shape, because I had been working out in anticipation of spring training. Besides that, Dr. Hyde separated the abdominal muscles to get to the appendix, rather than cutting through them. Recovering from surgically-severed muscles is a long process.

This way, he said, I should be up and around in three to four weeks. "Why?" I asked.

"Why? Because of the trauma of the operation. That's standard. You might be able to shave off a day or two if you're careful. You can join the team a week or two late in Vero Beach."

"I don't have three or four weeks," I said. "How soon can I be up and around?"

"You can walk whenever you feel up to it, but you shouldn't do anything strenuous for awhile."

"Why?"

"So you don't reopen the incision and aggravate the wound."

"But you're just talking about a surface wound, right? I'm not going to hurt anything inside?"

"Right. But if you reopen the scar, you could become infected."

"But that's the only danger?"

He nodded. I was being obnoxious, but I wanted to

know what the risks were. I was not going to lie in a hospital bed with an "owie" when my teammates were in spring training. This was an important time for us with new players and the nucleus of a potentially great team. It was crucial to me that I be there from the beginning, and that I was healthy. I didn't want to show up weak or unable to perform.

Within twenty-four hours after surgery, I was walking the halls with my IV pole. The next day the IV was removed and I began doing sit-ups, modified jumping jacks, stretching, and aerobics. I also sneaked out to walk and run the fire escape stairs. I was scolded, lectured, and warned by doctors and nurses, but I felt I knew my own body.

Four days after the operation I was discharged and speeding toward full workouts and complete recovery. I made the plane to spring training, and while they wouldn't let me pitch batting practice the first day, by the second day I was throwing in earnest. I never looked back.

So, what makes me like that, a person who asks "why?" A person who disdains what the textbooks say? A person who knows what's right for his body, who knows how to work out, and who will persist at all costs toward a goal?

I have to start with my dad and mom, Orel Hershiser III and Millie. My parents are great people who know both how to have fun and to work hard. My dad is *very* competitive. He is generous and a gentleman, but in everything he does, he wants to win. It didn't surprise me that the business he co-owned grew quickly over the years to be a very profitable enterprise. He sold his interest and retired at 51, a year after his goal. A few years ago, when I signed my first million-dollar deal, a friend asked my dad, "How does it feel to have a son making more money than you?"

Dad smiled and said, "I'll let you know if it ever happens."

Dad played to win—at cards with us kids, wrestling on the floor, or even just playing with his friends. Sometimes he would compete only with himself. I saw that side of him even in how he cleaned the garage. He took care of every detail and put everything in its place. When he assembled one of our toys, he became frustrated if the factory-drilled holes were not lined up or if pieces were missing. "The guy who did this job wasn't concentrating," he would complain.

We had a work ethic around our house. Katie, Gordie, Judd, and I weren't slaves; but there was a Saturday morning regimen for cleaning the house, and we worked as a family. We all had our individual chores. We knew what was expected of us in quality and speed, and we all met back at noon for lunch. We went through stages when we complained or wanted to put off our work, but we got nowhere with that.

"I'm sorry you don't like it," Dad would say, "but this is how the world works. You have to work, so get to work." He wasn't being mean. He was simply realistic. We learned good work habits from that, though we kid Judd that I was raised on hamburger and he was raised on steak. Everybody thinks their baby brother has it easier than they did, and since Dad's business grew through the years, it seemed life *was* easier for the younger ones. But they had to work, too.

We were commended and rewarded when we did a

good job, and we got a pat on the back even when we had to do something again. Mom or Dad might say, "The stairs look good, Orel, but you need to work a little harder in the corners, okay?"

To save herself countless trips up and down the stairs, Mom put clean clothes on the steps. Whoever was on his way up was expected to deliver them to the proper rooms. If we ignored them too often, we heard about it. There were right and wrong ways to do things. Dad was a perfectionist, and some of that rubbed off on us. We inherited the competitive spirit, too. Katie played college volleyball on scholarship, Gordie pitches in the Dodger farm system, and Judd earned a golf scholarship.

Because of that type of training and upbringing, I don't mind pain, and I don't mind work. I'm able to push myself past the point of working out just enough to get by. I want to be the best I can be, and I'm willing to pay the price. I don't make a big deal of it. It's internal.

I'm also an obsessive house cleaner. If we have company coming and Jamie asks me to straighten up the garage, I might clean that thoroughly and then start on kitchen drawers, closets, you name it, throwing away more than Jamie wants to get rid of. Company will be here in an hour, and I'm engaged in a major cleaning operation.

One other trait I got from my dad was the habit of asking why. I'm not talking about being curious about everything. The "why" my dad and I ask is really a "why not?" When someone makes a statement like "No one will ever break Bob Beamon's long jump record," Dad immediately says, "Why? How can you make a statement like that? Beamon did it. Why couldn't someone else do it? Couldn't those same elements of the right athlete, the right atmosphere, and the right technique ever come together again?"

He's not badgering. He likes discussions like that. And he always wants to know why someone feels the way he does. If the weatherman predicts rain and someone says, "There goes our golf date tomorrow," Dad will say, "Why? Does the weatherman have to be right? We don't know what tomorrow will be like. The storm may pass through. Let's plan on playing and see if it works out."

When you think about it, that's a tremendously positive philosophy of life.

He also instilled in me a stubborn, never-give-up attitude. I could be losing a table tennis match 20–3, but I would fight for every point until it was over. Besides the fact that I'll never come back and win if I don't, I also want to be a good sport and provide the better player with the best competition I can offer. I at least make him earn the victory. Dad would say, "Why *can't* you come back? Do you think no one's ever come back from that kind of a deficit before? Keep trying until it's over."

When I was young, my dad called me "Little O," and that was special to me. Jamie and I call Orel Leonard V "Quinton," Latin for *fifth*. The parents in our family are proud to pass the name along but sensitive enough to help the kids live with it by giving them nicknames.

Some of my fondest memories are of the Little League diamond we played on. Mom and Dad were active in every aspect from preparation of the fields and uniforms and organizing the teams to selling concessions, coaching, and umpiring. I remember my dad coming off the road after a sales trip, taking off his suit coat, getting on the umpire's gear, and officiating a game in his suit pants.

When we moved to Southfield, Michigan, from Buffalo—where I was born—Dad got me into tee ball a year earlier than normal. I was ready. I played ball all the time and learned to throw and hit and run properly by the time I was seven. At eight I entered the Personna Baseball Contest. I had torn up the tee ball league at seven, then fell off a little before I got glasses in mid-season the next year. Soon it appeared I had the skills to compete in the contest that called for running, throwing, and hitting.

I won the local event, and when my scores were compared to those from other states in our region, I was selected to go for the finals at Yankee Stadium in New York. It was while walking into that historic stadium on a crisp, windy night that I decided I wanted to be a big league baseball player. It was a thrill I remember as if it were yesterday. I was amazed at how puny my hits and throws seemed in that cavernous park. I hit a ball off the tee that seemed to go nowhere, and I wondered how a person could ever grow big and strong enough to hit a ball all the way into the outfield, let alone over the fence.

I finished third in the nation in the Personna contest and carried home a huge trophy, but the feeling of having been in that stadium stayed with me even longer than the thrill of my success.

When I was twelve we moved to Canada for a year, and I learned to play hockey the way it was meant to be played. When we moved to Cherry Hill, New Jersey, playing hockey helped me make new friends.

When I tried out for the varsity baseball team my first year at Cherry Hill East High School, I was deeply disappointed to be assigned to the freshman team. To me that was like being cut twice, once to the junior varsity, and again to the freshman team. It was unusual for a freshman to make the varsity, but that was my goal. As a sophomore I made the junior varsity team, but I wasn't satisfied till I finally made the varsity as a junior. I was tired of hearing about potential. I wanted to play, to compete, to contribute.

I played baseball all through high school, mostly pitching and playing shortstop. I was not the best player on my team the way most future big leaguers are, but I loved the game and the competition, and I was driven to get the most out of myself.

I was still learning from Dad, too. He always pushed me to succeed, and clearly, winning was a priority. But he also encouraged me to learn from losses. Once it's over and there's nothing more you can do about it, evaluate it, pick it apart, benefit from it. That philosophy has served me well.

By the time I was in high school my dad's business was doing well, but I was still expected to work. I pumped gas at the corner station for several years, and I worked in my dad's printing plant several summers, too.

I chose Bowling Green State University in Ohio for college because they had a good baseball program and were in a good athletic conference—the Mid-American. I had no idea when I made that choice that my parents would be moving back to Michigan. They would be close enough for emergencies and far enough (a couple of hours) that I had to live on campus.

I looked forward to college. I wasn't quite 18, but I felt a world of opportunity at my feet. I had no idea how much I leaned on my parents, or that I didn't have a clue how to live apart from them. I was about to painfully find out.

8

AWOL

When I started college in the fall of 1976, I thought I was independent. I didn't realize I had borrowed my values, my boundaries, and my rules from my parents. Though I should have known better, I thought I was ready to make my own decisions. As soon as I got to Bowling Green (as a Selling and Sales Marketing major), I felt free of the burden of having others making my decisions for me.

I was a know-it-all, and I thought I could take care of anything. If I didn't want to go to class, I didn't go. I believed I'd still make the baseball team in the spring. If I felt like playing pool instead of going to class, that's what I did. Another day I might sleep in because I stayed out too late the night before and had too many beers with the guys.

I somehow slid through the first semester, all the while lying through my teeth to my parents. I told them my classes were going well, that it was tough but I was doing all right. But in the Spring everything fell apart. It was time for baseball, but I was academically ineligible. My girlfriend broke up with me. And I wasn't prepared for finals. I panicked.

71

Everything at Bowling Green registered failure with me. I couldn't run my own life. I couldn't succeed with my girlfriend. I couldn't succeed in class. I couldn't play baseball. I had failed at every turn. The only place that appealed to me was where I had been happiest: Cherry Hill, New Jersey.

How could I face my parents, whom I loved and respected? I didn't want to do anything to hurt them or cause them to worry. I didn't know what to do or where to turn. I left a note for my roommate, and I left. I hitchhiked. While my classmates were taking their final exams, I was fleeing, and feeling worse by the mile.

I wasn't even old enough to realize that I was screaming for help. When I turned up missing, the news would get back to my parents; they would be worried sick, and I couldn't let that go on for long. I would never make Cherry Hill, and even if I had, there wasn't anything my old friends could have done for me to get me out of that mess.

I stopped at a hotel in mid-Pennsylvania and worked up the courage to make the toughest phone call of my life. There was no more sham now. I was the prodigal son, returning, admitting failure, and asking for help. I knew I had disappointed them terribly, and that hurt the most. To this day I often avoid confrontation and put off telling someone something they don't want to hear—though the silence is worse—because I so hate to disappoint anyone.

The conversation with my dad was mostly tears from my end, and I got the message that I'd better get home as soon as possible because "you've done a number on your mother." I was eager to get home. I was scared to be in charge of my own life, because if I was in charge, then I had to take the blame. I was willing to accept the blame for this fiasco, but now I wanted to regroup. I needed my parents' forgiveness and counsel. There would be no more snowing them. I was what I was and I had done what I had done.

Running away had been the same as admitting from the first that I couldn't cope. It was just a long-distance way of saying that I couldn't do it, that I had to leave. I had been too proud to say it, but eventually I had to.

Gratefully, I was welcomed home with open arms. It wasn't until I was nurtured back to normalcy and could sort out my problems that my parents talked to me about solutions. They enrolled me in summer school at Bowling Green and insisted that I apply myself and get back on track. I was capable; I just hadn't buckled down. I breezed through summer school with good grades and matured just seeing how I could take control of my own life. I had it in me to be a good student. But I had to apply the principles I had learned at home and exercise discipline in my life. Yes, I could make my own decisions, but I would reap the benefits or pay the price depending on their soundness.

After summer school I played on a team that won the All American Amateur Baseball Association national championship. I started the title game. But I had to wonder if I would ever be on a team that won a bigger game than that.

By my junior year at Bowling Green, I had grown three inches and added some weight. Overnight I had become a different athlete. Though I looked skinny, I was rangy and strong. I was a hard worker, competitive, and intense. I added five miles an hour to my fastball, made the traveling team, and finally saw success on the horizon. I didn't know how much success lay in store, but I was going after it.

My childhood dream to play big league baseball reappeared. I showed people I could compete at the college level, finishing the season with a 6-2 record and making the all-conference team. Local big league scouts visited every game and talked to me and my coach, Don Pervis. When there were no fans on a cold day, there would still usually be a couple of guys with stop watches and one with a radar gun.

I made the mistake of filling out a pro draftability questionnaire without knowing what they were looking for. I should have made it clear that I was gung-ho for going pro as soon as I could. I expressed an interest in staying in school and was noncommittal enough about other things that I'm sure my draftability went down.

I had the worst label a ballplayer can have: I had potential. To me that just meant I hadn't reached a level other people thought I should. I hated that with a passion. Everybody said I had a good curve, a decent fastball, and mediocre control. "But he's got a lot of potential."

I had an idea I might be taken in the 1979 amateur draft, but I had no idea which round or which team. I was excited and hopeful, but I didn't want to set myself up for a big letdown. I waited by the phone at my apartment on draft day, having told my parents that "if the Phillies or the Dodgers draft me, I think I want to turn pro." We had season tickets to Phillies games when we lived in Cherry Hill, so they were my hometown team. I'd always been impressed with what I'd heard about the Dodger minor league system, so Los Angeles was also high on my list.

What I didn't expect was to be drafted in the very first round. Though the call came from the San Diego Padres—not one of my choices—I couldn't ignore the fact that they thought enough of me to pick me first. I called my dad. We were thrilled and couldn't wait to see what they offered. First round picks were usually reserved for very well-known players at schools in the South or West where they play baseball almost year round.

I was so high I could hardly stand it. I looked for some of my friends to share the news with, but I couldn't find anybody. When they started showing up a little later, their reaction was strange. Some acted as if they didn't know what to say. Their congratulations sounded hollow. Others seemed to be fighting smiles. I didn't know if they were jealous or what.

Finally, it dawned on me. I had not been drafted by anyone yet. The call from the Padres had really been a call from my frat brothers. They had pulled off a royal practical joke, and I had fallen for it completely. I assured them it was funny and that I could take it, but you can imagine the disappointment.

Later, much later, I was drafted by the Los Angeles Dodgers in the 17th round. Nobody would kid about that. It wasn't first, but it was something. Best of all, it was Los Angeles. They were taking a chance on me because I had the kind of physique that could produce a good prospect if I filled out. My fastball was in the low 80s at that time, but they assumed that if I got bigger and stronger and learned technique, I could develop a big league fastball. They were taking a chance on natural, raw ability and what they thought they could teach me. They rated my competitiveness very high.

In one year I had gone from being a sophomore who didn't make the traveling squad to the ace of the staff. Boyd Bartley, a Dodger scout, came to our home in June to present the offer to my dad and me. I wouldn't be 21 until September, so Dad would have to give me permission and sign the contract.

"We would assign you to Clinton, Iowa," Mr. Bartley said. "From there the future is up to you. You have the chance to grow and develop and work your way up the ladder to play in the big leagues. You have the chance of a lifetime to pitch at Dodger Stadium someday. We're prepared to offer you ten thousand dollars to sign."

My dad and I excused ourselves and talked it over in another room. "Even if we try to negotiate this, how much are we going to get?" he said. "A 17th round pick can't demand a large amount. The question is, do you really want to become a professional baseball player?"

He was treating me like an adult, and I appreciated it. I was caught up in the excitement of being drafted and I wanted this more than I had ever wanted anything in my life. "Dad," I said, "I want to try. I just want to try."

My mother came in from the kitchen. "What are you guys going to do?"

"The kid wants to try," Dad said. "Let's let him try. He can always go back to school."

What we didn't know when we agreed to the deal, of course, was that of 100 similar prospects, 96 fail.

Fewer than 4 percent put on a big league uniform and see spring training or even record a few at bats in the bigs. One percent of the best amateur baseball players in the country, those who sign pro contracts, make enough money in baseball to support their families. I was going to be that one in a hundred, but I'm glad I didn't know the odds then.

9

ARGYLES, LOW AND AWAY

When I look back on my minor league career, a jumble of impressions hits me. I was one of about ten new draftees added to the Clinton, Iowa, Class A club. Fresh meat. We were coming and other guys were going, their dreams dashed. I'll never forget taking the locker of a guy who left with his belongings in his bag, his eyes vacant.

"Hey!" someone hollered at him. "The new guy's gonna need your hat and stirrups."

Without a word he fished them out and tossed them to me. I wondered if I'd be doing the same thing someday, heading home with a memory, a story for the grandkids about a chance I once had with the Dodgers.

More important than anything else in my minor league career were three friends I met. One I have since lost track of and would like to hook up with again some time. Another I have promised to love and live with for the rest of my life. The other has promised to love me and let me live with Him forever.

Butch Wickensheimer was a teammate at Clinton. He intrigued me. When the rest of us were out having a good time, he was relaxing, reading his Bible, staying sober. A nice guy. We kidded him about being religious, but he wasn't obnoxious about it. He didn't condemn anybody or corner them and preach at them. He just didn't let them interfere with his own convictions. On the team bus, he would try to sit under a light that was working so he could read his Bible.

I asked him what he saw in it. "Everything," he told me. "It's God's gift to man. It tells how much He loves us and how we can know Him."

That sounded all right. I had a Bible. It was in the bottom drawer of my dresser at home, where it had been all my life. I went to church on Easter and Christmas, and they had Bibles in the pews, so I didn't need to take mine. When did I read it? Never. I believed in God and Adam and Eve and heaven. People went to heaven if they were good. Christians were good.

Butch had a different idea. He didn't push me, but when I asked, he would explain what the Bible said about heaven. Good people don't go there. Forgiven people do. There was nothing I could do to qualify for heaven. I was a sinner, just like everybody else. The only perfect Person who ever lived was Jesus, and He had taken the punishment for sin. The only way to God was through Jesus. You had to receive Him, make Him your Savior.

"Where does it say that?" I asked.

"John 14:6 and Ephesians 2:8–9," Butch said. When no one was around, I looked those up in a Gideon Bible in the hotel room. It took me half an hour to find them, because I didn't know how the Bible was arranged. Sure enough, that's what it said. I wanted to argue with Butch about it, but I didn't want the other guys to see me talking to him too much. They might get the wrong idea. They might put me in the Christian athlete category.

I played devil's advocate with Butch. I asked him everything from how he knew there was a God and how he knew the Bible was really from God to what happens to children if they die before they become Christians. I was looking for an out. I needed a reason to say it wasn't for me. If I could find some major problem with it, some big inconsistency, I could say that I had made a decision. That decision would be no, and I could quit thinking about it, quit talking about it.

When the season was over and I went back home, I dug my Bible out and read more. "This is what Butch reads everyday," I told myself. "Amazing."

I had made a decent start in my career, winning four and losing none, and Butch and I had both been selected to attend the Arizona Instructional League in the fall. That was a big deal to me, because only a few players from each minor league team were assigned. I asked if Butch could be one of my roommates at the Buckaroo Hotel in Scottsdale. Out there I quizzed him more and more. How could this be? What about that? Explain this. Answer that. He was patient, and he was consistent. His answers always came from the Bible.

I finally realized that Butch was limited. He could answer questions and he could point out verses, but he couldn't convince me. He couldn't make the decision for me. I was going to have to accept

Christianity or reject it. More specifically, Butch explained, it was Christ I was deciding about. Was He just a man, a good teacher like so many say? And how could He be called a good teacher if He Himself claimed to be God and wasn't? What kind of a teacher is that?

I wasn't a big time scoundrel, but I knew my life would change if I bought into this. It was no minor matter. Did it make sense to me? Could I accept what I understood and take the rest by faith? Or was there still a way out? Could I point to disasters and catastrophes and somehow blame God and ease my conscience?

Butch said God loved me and wanted a relationship with me. What could *that* mean? I could know God? God could know me? God was perfect and I wasn't. I was just a guy, and He was, well, God. How could I relate to Him? Butch said Jesus was the answer. I could relate to Him because even though He was perfect, He had also become a Man. He was the bridge. He paid for my sin. If I could accept that and believe in Christ, then I could be forgiven and know I was going to heaven.

He had paid for my sin. He was the bridge. He was perfect for me. If I could accept that and believe in Christ, then I could be a child of God.

It took a long time to sink in. Sometimes, just when I was thinking it sounded pretty good, I would catch myself. "You're not really thinking about this, are you?" I'd ask myself. "Are you starting to believe it?" I would be one of the guys for a while, and then I would gravitate back toward Butch, asking more and more questions.

I almost wore out the poor guy with all my

skepticism and badgering. Down deep I knew it was my decision. There was no more to ask. I was tired of making up questions he couldn't answer just so I could prove him wrong and not have to believe. I had to do something about the sin problem that he showed me in Romans 3:23. Since there was nothing I could personally do about it, I had to make a decision about John 3:16. If all have sinned, I'm included. And if those who believe in Jesus can live forever, well, the only thing left to decide was whether or not I believed that.

One September night at the Buckaroo, I was the only one in the room. I pulled out the Gideon Bible and was reading the book of John. My mind was racing. Do I believe in God? Yes. Do I believe the Bible is God's message to man? Yes. Do I believe what the Bible says? Yes. That all have sinned? Yes. That nothing I can do can save me from my sin? Yes. That Jesus already did it for me and that He is the only way to God? Yes. Do I want Christ in my life? Do I want to become a Christian?

I slipped off the bed and knelt beside it. How does one go about praying? I didn't know. I figured if God was God, He would understand if I just told Him what was on my mind. I said, "God, I don't know everything about you. I don't think I ever will. But I know I'm a sinner and I know I want to be forgiven. I know I want Christ in my life, and I want to go to heaven. I want to become a Christian. With that, I accept You. Amen."

No tears, no lightning, no wind, no visions. I just got back on the bed and continued to read the Bible. What a relief! I knew I had done the right thing. I had stepped from skepticism to belief. God had forgiven me and Christ was in me, and the character He had already built into me affected the type of a Christian I would become. I was an all or nothing kind of a guy. This wasn't something I had simply taken care of and gotten out of the way. I was into this all the way. I wanted to quit pretending to be happy about other players' success when secretly I wanted to be the only one doing well. I wanted to quit living a lie and be genuinely thrilled when a teammate was called up to the big leagues.

Almost immediately, God gave me a genuine love and compassion for people. I could be happy for someone else without suffering myself. God impressed upon me that He would take care of me and love me no matter what. Whether I made the big leagues and became rich and famous and had everything the world has to offer or I failed at baseball, He would be there.

When Butch got in, I told him, "I accepted the Lord tonight, and I really feel good about it."

He was as matter-of-fact as I was. I know he was thrilled for me, but in his own way he simply let me know what the next steps were. He recommended a lot of Bible reading, especially in passages that were meaningful to him when he was a new Christian. He said I should get into a Bible study, start going to a church that believed and taught the Bible, spend time with other Christians, and start telling other people about my decision.

My faith was very personal. It meant everything to me. I checked against the Bible every new thing I heard. I let the Bible speak to me. When I went home at the end of the instructional league, I was impressed with how much Christmas meant to me, for the first time in my life.

In the instructional league I had started getting a picture of how many fine pitchers were in the Dodger system. At my first spring training in Vero Beach, Florida, early in 1980, reality set in. A dozen second basemen took groundballs, one at a time and then back in line. Sixty pitchers shared a half dozen mounds, and all of them looked bigger and stronger and faster and more accurate and more mature. I realized that every one of them had been told what I was told: "You have a chance to pitch on the mound at Dodger Stadium someday." Only a handful of us would.

I would make a fairly typical progression from Clinton to San Antonio to Albuquerque and finally to Los Angeles. I had hot streaks when I looked like the best thing that had come along in years and cold streaks that made me want to go AWOL like I had at Bowling Green. Once it took my coaches to convince me they wanted me to stay around. They told me I had big league potential—there was that word again. But when you can't find the plate and your ERA is in the stratosphere, you believe coaches are only being polite. Maybe they didn't want to have to explain how a prospect disappeared overnight. I couldn't attribute to my encouragers a pure motive; it was beyond me to believe they could really see past my inadequacy.

And perhaps they *were* just trying to be nice and keep me around until it was time to thin out the rosters. It turned out, of course, that they were right about what they said, regardless of its sincerity.

After spring training in 1980, I was assigned to the

double-A club in San Antonio, Texas. I had my ups
and downs as a pitcher there, but I grew spiritually
too. I began attending church and also discovering
that God likes to answer prayer.

I was a normal young adult, lonely, eager for
companionship, and attracted to women. I knew it
would be wrong to sleep around like so many
athletes do away from home. Yet I didn't know
anyone who would understand my values, my new
morals. On June 2 I put on my prayer list a request
that God would put a Christian girl into my life.

I had completely forgotten about that three nights
later when I saw a pretty girl at a party who seemed
to be looking at me when I looked at her. When I
finally introduced myself to her, she thought I was
joking.

I liked her smile and her laugh. "I'm Jamie Byars.
What's your real name?"

"That is my real name," I assured her.

"You must be one of the baseball players."

I nodded. "I play for the San Antonio Dodgers."

She told me her father was an executive for the
company that owned the team. She was on her way
home from college and had come to the party with
her mother. I found out later that she had almost not
come because she didn't want to "meet a bunch of
jocks."

"When are you going to become a professional?"

I laughed. "Just because I'm not in the big leagues
yet doesn't mean I don't get paid to play."

We chatted for a long time and discovered we were
both Christians. I was still not reminded of my
prayer request. I spent more time at the party with
Jamie and her mother, and when the evening ended,

they offered me a ride home. Jamie's mother insisted on being dropped off first. That was a good opportunity, but I had made the mistake of not taking a bathroom break all evening. Here was a chance to really get to know a nice Christian girl, but I was in crisis. I wanted to get home.

When we got to my place, I wasn't too cool about asking for her number. I just blurted it out. "What's your phone number? I'll call you sometime." She gave it to me, I shook her hand, said, "I gotta go (which was truer than she knew), I'll see you," and went inside. She told her mother I seemed like a nice guy, and *very* polite.

The next day the Dodgers left on a 10-day road trip, but I knew one thing: As soon as we got back, I was calling this girl. I invited her to a game, which went far into extra innings, which she sat through alone in the cold. For three of the next six weeks, I was on the road. But when I was in town, we were together, talking every minute. Well, almost every minute. I told her I could get serious. She told me, "Let's just have a good time."

But in six weeks, we thought we knew each other well. On August 1 we were engaged. She visited me in Arizona that fall, and when instructional league was over, I got a job and an apartment in San Antonio. Just before spring training, in February of 1981, we were married. We look back now and know we hardly knew each other. But it was right, and our life together has been wonderful.

Jamie has been with me all the way. I can never forget a period when I seemed to lose touch with my mechanics. My release point eluded me, and I was frustrated, not pitching well, worried about my future. She offered to catch me, but of course she couldn't catch a baseball if I threw it hard. Instead I threw a pair of socks. A *Sports Illustrated* writer called those pitches "argyles, low and away."

Jamie teases that that was just one of the many sacrifices she's had to make over the years, and there's more than humor there. Our goal from the beginning was to see me make the big leagues, but neither of us could envision what my career has become. And while it is in many ways a dream come true, we couldn't have predicted the pressures that come with it either.

10

MAKING IT

Some might think Jamie has the best of everything. After all, she's married to a famous person who has given her financial security. I don't want any sympathy, but there are negative sides to everything. We look back on our days in the early minors, when we were struggling to make ends meet, as some of the happiest days of our lives.

Jamie is a single parent during a lot of the baseball season. She is in charge and has to take care of everything. And when I'm home, I'm not always really home. There are speaking engagements and appearances, games to prepare for, questions to answer, people to see, deals to decide on. I wouldn't pretend there aren't rewards to go along with the hassle, but with privilege always comes responsibility and more time demands. That puts pressure on a family. With two little boys at home, we want more than anything to be free of distractions that would make us less effective parents.

When it was just the two of us and we were starting out, the pressures were there, but they were

different. I was obsessed with my goal, and that was
to make it. No minor leaguer wants anything more.
The big leagues is the goal, and nothing short of that
is acceptable. Some discover they are good enough
only for A ball, others double-A, others triple-A. The
truly frustrated are those who fall somewhere between triple-A and the majors. There's little joy in
leading a triple-A league in hitting or pitching, yet
not being able to produce in the big leagues.

My goal at every level was to reach the next,
knowing that some day my break would come. My
faith had rescued me from the jealousy and backbit-
ing that normally went with seeing a teammate
move up faster than I did. But still, my goal was to
make the Dodgers.

Spiritually, I had other goals. Jamie and I were
happy to find a good church that was active and
enthusiastic. We wanted to grow individually and as
a couple. Our marriage had, and has, the usual rough
spots that most couples endure, but a truly Christian marriage is different.

The marriage with Christ at its head consists of a
man and a woman who are unwaveringly committed to each other, regardless what might be said or
done in anger or a weak moment. While we might
express ourselves bluntly in frustration, separation
or divorce is not even part of our vocabulary. That's
a bedrock security that both of us know and enjoy. It
allows us to be honest with each other, working
through our problems without fear of losing each
other.

Personally, we want to live and breathe Christ
without embarrassing Him. I had to learn what the
Bible meant when one of the writers said we should

"pray without ceasing." I've come to know that feeling, not of having my eyes closed or being on my knees or having my hands folded, but rather to be in tune with God at every moment. I can be in contact with God, open to His thoughts, aware of His presence, all the time—even when I'm talking with someone, playing a game, or whatever. There are times to pray specifically and more formally, but to me, praying continually means being in constant contact with God.

That can be difficult for the conscience. If I'm angry or spiteful or do something I know God would not approve of, I tend to know it immediately. That allows me to acknowledge what's wrong, ask His forgiveness, and move on.

I'm not one to wear my faith on my sleeve. Christians can do a disservice to unbelievers by being obnoxious or judgmental. I'm a chapel leader and have been since my second year in the minors. People know where I'm coming from without my having to harp on it all the time. I know that the message of Christ offends because it calls sin sin and says we all are sinners. There's no way to soften that truth. It's jarring and can alienate people until they begin to realize that it's true. My pushing it down everyone's throat will not make it any easier for them to investigate what it's all about.

I just tell people about God naturally, when opportunities arise or when I'm asked. It's amazing how many people notice when you tend to be straight. If you're not a carouser, not a womanizer, not foul-mouthed, not a gossip, it gets around. When I was a young Christian, I struggled with my image. I didn't want to be out of it, but I was soon pegged as religious. I wasn't included, and sometimes I got teased. During winter ball one year I told Jamie that I felt ostracized almost from the beginning. Guys would call me Reverend or Preacher, and if they swore in front of me they apologized. I didn't want that. If I could be a good influence, fine. If I was different from people who didn't care about God, that was okay. But I wasn't trying to be a goody-two-shoes.

Jamie and I were good for each other because we had both come to Christ as young adults and had been freed from self-centeredness. It isn't that we never again battled pride or ego; that's very difficult for a person in the public eye who receives adulation from people on the street. But Jamie's goal had been to be an excellent student and an opera singer. Mine was to make the big leagues. We were obsessive and perfectionistic, which can be valuable traits if your motive and goal are right. But when it made us drive ourselves for our own sakes, it was wrong.

Jamie says she felt tremendous relief and freedom when she quit worrying about whether she was the most talented or the smartest or the best looking and relaxed in the knowledge that she was accepted by God. Her motive became to do her best to bring credit to Him, not to herself. I was still obsessive and a perfectionist, but my motive was to succeed so that God would get the glory.

We're far from perfect. We fail. There are people who may think we are insincere or who think we're judgmental. I can't defend myself against people who say I'm phony. Only my family, my true friends, and I know who I really am inside. I'll have to answer for that someday. I can only do and be what I think God wants me to do and be. I never want to embarrass Him or bring Him shame.

My faith has been a balancing agent in my life. Christ thrills me with who I am in Him, and reminds me gently who I am not. When I suffer, I know I'm still loved. When I'm on top of the world, I remember that my accomplishments mean nothing in light of eternity. The biggest surprise to me was to discover that Christ is real. He's not some nebulous concept, some idea or system or approach or philosophy. He's a Person, someone I can know.

And He knows me. How do I know? Because while He changed me from sinner to forgiven-sinner, He also realigned my motives. I still had the same character and personality, but my mind was renewed because I now wanted to do what He wanted me to do. The obsession and perfectionism I had used to promote myself was now redirected. I wanted to be the best baseball player I could be, and now that my motives were right, I was free to enjoy my pursuit rather than be frustrated by it. I've seen players worry so much about how they're doing that they are no longer effective.

If anything, I became more dedicated to paying the price, to working out, to listening, to learning. I wanted to soak up all the baseball knowledge I could. *Sport Magazine* has called me "the smartest pitcher in the big leagues," which is embarrassing and impossible to prove. But I don't apologize for wanting to be a smart pitcher. There are plenty of other ones around, and I admire them. I admire any professional who feels obligated to earn his salary by giving his all, not just every time he's on the mound or at the plate, but during every minute of mental and physical preparation.

One of the great disappointments in my career came in the spring of 1983 after I'd risen from A to double-A and triple-A and then won the Mulvey Award as the top Dodger rookie in spring training. When Tommy Lasorda told me I was heading back to Albuquerque for the start of the season, I wondered what more a guy had to do. If the best rookie couldn't make the big club, who could?

I knew better than to let it get me down and destroy my confidence. I was all the more determined to do well in the Pacific Coast League. I thought the decision to send me back was wrong, but I had fought through such disappointments before, in both high school and college. I had my faith, and I had my wife. Jamie is so good at times like that. Even today, if I have a bad outing, I know I can just lie in bed with my arm around her and be able to either talk about my frustrations or not say anything.

There are times when she wants to get inside my head and know what I'm thinking. But she also knows there are times when I don't want to talk. I just want to think, to mull over a mistake, to solidify in my mind how I will avoid it in the future. If I dwell upon my mistakes, the worst thing she can do is to try to gloss them over or explain them away or tell me they aren't so bad. When your entire professional life is devoted to one thing, and you fail at it, it *is* bad. It isn't life or death, but it's serious. I never want to take it lightly.

And Jamie never does. Arguing with me and trying to convince me that everything is okay would irritate me and make me defensive. I would insist that things are not all right and that they are more serious than people think. But instead Jamie just tells me she loves me and is proud of me, no matter what. Even when I don't respond, or can't respond, that is a healing moment. Knowing she's behind me and trusts me and believes in me makes me a better man. And knowing she would love me even if I hadn't made it to the big leagues makes me a secure husband.

When I finished third in the Pacific Coast League in saves and seventh in earned run average in 1983, I had earned my promotion to the Dodgers. I joined them near the end of the season and pitched eight innings in eight games as a reliever. I never wanted to see Albuquerque again, at least not as a baseball player.

Being a big leaguer was the fulfillment of my dream, but I wasn't through learning yet. What a place to study the game! I even irritated my new teammates because I liked to sit on the other end of the bench, with Tommy, Perry, and Monty Basgall (our infield coach).

I loved to listen to Tommy and the coaches discuss situations and strategy. Eventually, I felt free to join in, offering opinions, asking why certain moves were made or not made. When I said something stupid, I heard about it, but that didn't bother me. I still loved it. They sent me on errands occasionally, and when I came back past the players at the other end of the bench some would say, "Hey, Senator, are you running for re-election?" But I wasn't trying to get in good with the coaches. It bothered me that some guys thought that; but I knew it wasn't true, and I wasn't going to quit just because of peer pressure.

I really wanted to be a student of the game. Since early in my minor league days, I had heard former players say with regret, "I wish I knew then what I know now." I wanted to avoid that feeling at all costs. That has become the theme of my career.

It was great to become a valuable member of the pitching staff after Tommy's "Sermon on the Mound" in 1984. Jamie was pregnant for the first time, and it was a relief to know I had my feet on the ground professionally.

We were the typical modern parents, going to natural childbirth classes and learning how to breathe during contractions and all that. Jamie went into labor the day before her birthday, and as the clock approached midnight, she was about to give birth. The doctor asked if she wanted to blow through her next several contractions and "have the baby born on your birthday?"

Between contractions Jamie yelled, "Let him have his own birthday!" Orel V was born November 24, 1984.

Fatherhood must have inspired me. In 1985 I was 19–3 with the best winning percentage in baseball (.864). I won my last eleven decisions, the longest winning streak for a Dodger pitcher in ten years. My 11–0 record and ERA of 1.08 at Dodger Stadium is still a single-season record for Los Angeles pitchers.

That season I pitched two one-hitters, a two-hitter, and a three-hitter, had a string of 22 consecutive scoreless innings, and once faced 29 batters over a three-game stretch without the ball being hit out of the infield. I finished third in the voting for the Cy Young Award. I felt good, and I felt lucky. If only I had known what I was doing, I might have had a chance to duplicate it the next year.

After that season my attorney, Robert Fraley, represented me in arbitration, and I was awarded a $1 million salary. In 1986 I was the same pitcher, trying just as hard, but the results were not the same. My ERA was still under 2.0 at the end of May, but I finished the season 14–14 with a 3.85 ERA. This time we lost in arbitration, and I took a twenty percent cut in pay. It wasn't based on my having had a .500 season, because I did the same in 1987 (16–16) and got a raise to $1.1 million (without having to go to arbitration).

Though my record didn't show it, I ranked among the league leaders in almost every pitching category in '87. I was first in innings pitched (264.2) and third in complete games (10), and made the all-star team for the first time. We averaged 4.01 runs per game when I pitched and scored three runs or less 15 times. I lost 8 one-run games that year. For the second year in a row, we finished fourth, and it was time to speak up. We needed more talent, more horses, if we were going to compete.

I felt good about my progress and even better about the advice I was getting from Robert, who was much more than a representative. He became a true friend, and his counsel on keeping my priorities straight was some of the best I ever got. He convinced me that the off-the-field opportunities I enjoyed (endorsements, appearances, commercials, and speaking engagements) were wholly dependent on how I did on the field. "All that will be gone if you don't perform. If you take those opportunities to the detriment of your game, your game will be gone and they will be gone too."

As a fellow Christian, Robert also talked about family life and priorities and that the measure of my career would be whether at the end I had something to show for it. "If when it's over, you have a solid marriage, a happy family, true friends, financial security appropriate to the level of income you have enjoyed, and respect in the community, then you will have been a success."

It's sad how many ballplayers, even some in high income brackets, leave the game with no security and a broken family.

I believe God prepared me for the kind of success I would have in 1988. I'm a late bloomer, and earlier in my career I might not have been able to handle being a Cy Young award winner, a playoff and Series MVP, and all that goes with it.

After my emergency appendectomy just before spring training, I never would have predicted a year like the one I enjoyed. But after seeing the talent the front office had rounded up during the off-season, I was privately optimistic about the potential of the team.

PART FOUR

THE SEASON

11

FOR THOSE MOMENTS

There are moments in baseball that just can't be beat. When every pitch makes a difference, when every decision is crucial, when the game can turn on one swing of the bat, one throw, one catch—those moments make it all worth it. I'll go through the workouts, the sweat, the blah games, the waiting, just to be there for those moments.

When a big league team is in the midst of a division pennant race, a league championship series, or a World Series, an entire season can be made or broken with one play. An injury, an error, poor judgment, and victory becomes defeat in an instant.

There were enough moments like that in the 1988 season to cover a career. In fact, had someone told me that everything that happened to the Dodgers and to me last year would occur over ten seasons, I couldn't have asked for more. That it all happened in fewer than fifty days has left me in shock. I sometimes wonder if it was a dream.

Is it possible that a team that suffered back-to-back fourth place finishes in 1986 and 1987 could make the deals and bring together the ingredients to make a run for the National League Western Division title? With lefthander Fernando Valenzuela suffering all year and eventually going on the disabled list, could the Dodgers defy the odds, surprise the experts, and win the championship? In the heat of the race, could I help carry the team with a string of consecutive scoreless innings longer than any one pitcher in history, pitch eight straight complete games, win 23, pitch five shutouts in a row, then go ten scoreless innings in another?

Though the regular season ended with my streak at 59 consecutive innings, could I add eight more in the playoffs? Could we beat the Mets after having lost 10 of 11 to them during the regular season? Could I be named MVP (Most Valuable Player) of the championship series? Could we go on, in spite of a rash of injuries that decimated our club, to win the World Series against a highly favored Oakland team? Could I become MVP in the Series too, win the National League Cy Young award and just about every other annual athletic honor I could think of?

See why I still find it hard to believe! I never had a superstar tag. I was competent. I had ability. At times I even showed flashes of brilliance. But who would have predicted this?

At the end of August, heading into my scheduled start against the Expos in Montreal, I was thrilled with my season and especially with the Dodgers' chances in the Western Division. We were six and a half games ahead of Houston. Here's a fast overview of the season t *hat point:

The front o   ·l been aggressive since long

before the season opener. Fred Claire, executive vice president for player personnel, had acquired short-stop Alfredo Griffin and relief pitchers Jay Howell and Jesse Orosco through trades with the Oakland Athletics and the Mets. Later he signed free agent Mike Davis, who had been a power hitter with Oakland.

It was, however, the signing of free agent Kirk Gibson, a long-time star for the Detroit Tigers, that added the final piece to our puzzle. He would hit before Pedro Guerrero and Mike Marshall to give us one of the most feared three-four-and-five combinations in the league.

No one knew the kind of a year Gibson would have. We could only hope. All he did was run up totals that made him the clear choice for National League MVP. But Kirk did more than lead us with his ability. He made it clear from the beginning that his only goal for the season was a world's championship. Here was a guy who could have played the big shot, insisted on special treatment, and treated the non-stars like dirt. But he didn't. He led by example. An indication of his attitude: "I'll take an 0 for 5 in a win over a 3 for 5 in a loss any day."

Kirk treated the reserves the same way he treated the starters. Mickey Hatcher, the ultimate utility man, started referring to himself and his reserve cohorts as the Stuntmen because of all the ways they sacrificed themselves to make the starters look good. We had no idea how important those guys would be to us during the year. They stepped in when necessary and played like starters. We could not have succeeded without them. Guys like Dave Anderson, Franklin Stubbs, Mike Sharperson, Tracy

Woodson, Demper, and Danny Heep carried us, especially when injuries plagued the starters. In Kirk Gibson's view, everyone was important to the total picture, from the clubhouse men to the bat boys. If you're working hard and you're part of the organization, you're a Dodger, and he treated you that way.

Gibson was a hard worker, showing up early for batting practice, berating himself when he made a mistake, cheering and going crazy when we succeeded. During spring training someone smeared eye black inside Gibby's cap, eager to see his reaction when his forehead was streaked. Kirk was furious. "No wonder this is a fourth place team," he fumed.

Some might think he overreacted, that he should have rolled with the punches, lightened up, been one of the guys. The fact is, he *was* one of the guys all year. His and Steve Sax's antics on and off the field, in the locker room, on the bus, everywhere we went, kept us loose and laughing. Saxy's impersonations of coaches, players, and fans were priceless.

At the time of the practical joke on Gibson, all we could think was that here was a guy who cared, really cared about winning. There was a time for work and a time for play, and this was a time for work. Suddenly it became cool to care, to pay the price, to win. No sitting back on our laurels, no relaxing with a big salary and celebrity status. If Kirk Gibson could hustle, we could all hustle.

From that point on, Kirk became our leader in spirit and in morale. We became a close-knit team, not in the rah-rah, artificial sense that some teams do. But we began to care about each other, to pull together, to strive for a common goal. Some of us had been vocal after two straight fourth-place finishes. I went on record that we didn't have the horses to make a run for the pennant and that I hoped the Dodgers would do something about it. Maybe that seemed disrespectful or brash, but now they had done it. They had made the deals. The horses were there. Now what were *we* going to do about it? It was time to put up or shut up.

The season opener was disappointing. After second baseman Steve Sax hit the first pitch of the season for a homer, we didn't score another run all day. Even with Fernando Valenzuela on the mound, we lost 5–1 to the Giants. We couldn't know then, of course, that that game would be characteristic of Freddie's season. It was painful for all of us to see such a fierce competitor suffer most of the year with a sore arm and finally have to sit out the playoffs and the Series.

Freddie's the kind of guy who makes me smile just to think of him. He's fun-loving and likes to pretend he doesn't understand English. We all know he understands more than he lets on. He communicates through body language—and his lasso. He can lasso a guy's trailing foot as he walks by. I know there's nothing he'd rather do than get healthy and return to top form. When I think of what we did in the World Series last year without him and Gibson and then I think of the addition of Eddie Murray, whom we picked up from the Baltimore Orioles—well, maybe in 1989 we won't be such a surprise to everyone.

In spite of our opening day loss, we won the next five straight, one over the Giants (my first start, a three-hit shutout) and four straight in Atlanta. I was National League Pitcher of the Month for April, tied for the league lead with five wins and no losses and an ERA of 1.56. We were 13–7, a half game behind the division-leading Houston Astros. Mike Scioscia (Sosh), a lifetime .263 hitter, started strong and led the league in hitting at .404. Though he finished the season hitting .257, he struck out only a dozen times in more than 400 at bats.

We gave evidence of being a solid team on the road, winning seven of our first nine away-games. More importantly, in fifteen tries against the competition in our own division, we had won eleven. By May 4, I was 6–0 with victories over Atlanta (3–1 and 3–2), San Francisco (10–3), New Orleans (6–4), and Pittsburgh (8–5). By May 11, we were 19–9 and had a three-game lead over the Astros. Then we hit a slump. We lost three in a row, two to the Pittsburgh Pirates (including my first loss, 7–4, on May 12), and one to the Phillies. We dropped five of our next eight games (including my second loss, 3–0 to Montreal, which allowed Houston to tie us for the lead).

I should have taken the year off against the Pirates. Had it not been for them, I probably would have won the ERA title. I gave up 7 earned runs in seven innings in that loss, 4 in five innings for another loss to them in July, and 3 more in six innings in an August loss. I was 1–3 against them for the year and gave up 16 earned runs in just under 25 innings for an ERA of almost 6!

In a tough late-May series against the Mets at home, we suffered more than just three straight losses. In the second game, shortstop Alfredo Griffin broke his right hand when a pitch got away from Dwight Gooden. Alfredo would miss 57 games.

Dave Anderson substituted for him and played some of the best shortstop I've ever seen. Andy hit .287 during that stretch and made just 4 errors in 63 games. We quickly realized how important it was to have someone who could step in and perform like that without missing a beat.

We lost our third straight to the Mets the day after Griffin's injury and found ourselves a game and a half behind the Astros. That would prove to be our worst standing of the year since our opening day loss. The next day we began a four-game winning streak with a 2–1, twelve-inning victory at Philadelphia. Those kinds of victories can really boost a club.

I need to say that I was hardly the lone successful pitcher for the Dodgers in 1988. Tim Leary's one-hit shutout of the Phillies on May 25 was the best pitched game of the season. He pitched complete games in 30 percent of his starts, ranking seventh in the league with nine complete games. He would finish sixth in strikeouts with 180 and second to me in shutouts with six (I had eight).

On May 26 we moved into first place for good with a ninth-inning, 3-run rally to beat the Phillies 10–8. Though we were only a half game ahead of Houston and five ahead of the Giants at the end of May, by the end of June we were five ahead of Houston and five-and-a-half ahead of the Giants. We won 10 of our last 12 during the month. On June 3 we had tied a record set by the New York Giants in 1931 when we had 22 singles and no extra base hits in a 13–5 victory over the Cincinnati Reds at Dodger Stadium.

One of the highlights in June was our bullpen,

which had 11 saves. Jay Howell proved to be a real stopper (five saves in six opportunities), and he would go on to finish eighth in the National League with 21 for the season. Alejandro Peña would lead the staff with 60 appearances and finish with 12 saves in 14 opportunities. (He had a 22-inning score-less streak from mid-June to mid-July.) Lefty Jesse Orosco finished with nine saves and a 2.72 ERA in 55 appearances. Our middle men, Brian Holton and Tim Crews, finished the year with marks of 7–3 (1.70) and 4–0 (3.14).

I was 5–1 in June with three complete games and one shutout, while Mike Marshall, John Shelby, and Dave Anderson all batted over .300. The Dodgers were confounding the pre-season prognosticators.

We should have gotten an idea of what the rest of the season and post-season would be like on July 6 when we enjoyed the first of several improbable finishes. Trailing the Cardinals 3–0 going into the bottom of the eighth, we exploded for 7 runs, the last 4 coming on Franklin Stubbs's grand slam. While we never dropped out of first place again, we did see a seven-game lead shrivel to a half game when we lost nine of eleven the last week of July and the first week of August. Then, with fifteen wins in our next twenty games, we surged back to six and a half games ahead. We had enjoyed four four-game win-ning streaks and one of five games before the all-star break. I personally had two six-game winning streaks and finished the first half of the season 13–4.

In an August 13 game against the San Francisco Giants at home, Tommy Lasorda ran out of right-handed pinch hitters and played a hunch, sending pitcher Tim Leary in to pinch hit with two out in the ninth. He hit a 3–2 pitch up the middle to drive in the winning run. It was his only pinch hitting role of the year, but for the season he hit .269 with three game-winning RBIs and a .300+ slugging percentage! That earned him the National League's Silver Bat Award as the top hitting pitcher.

We began the second half with six straight wins, but our longest streak of the season (seven) began, oddly enough, the day after one of my worst shellackings of the year. In a home game against the Giants on August 14, I was ripped for 8 runs in two innings (5 earned) for my seventh loss against 16 wins. San Francisco beat us 15–4 for their only win in a four-game series in Los Angeles.

Dodger minor league pitching supervisor Dave Wallace happened to be in town for meetings and noticed that I was opening up too soon with my front foot. The next day he mentioned it to me and I began working on it, unaware of how that little adjustment might affect the rest of the season.

Two days later the club traded Pedro Guerrero, our offensive leader for nine seasons, to St. Louis for John Tudor, one of the premier lefties in the league. He would go 2–1 in three starts the rest of the month with a 2.86 ERA.

My mechanical adjustment had an immediate effect, and I shut out the Expos 2–0 on August 19. The next day we had another one of those incredible finishes as Kirk Gibson danced off second base in the bottom of the ninth with the score tied at 3. When a wild pitch skipped past the Expos' catcher, Gibby was off and running. As he rounded third he decided to go for it. The throw was late from the catcher to the pitcher covering, and Kirk scored the winning run.

Our pitching was becoming solid. Rookie starter Tim Belcher came into his own in August, going 3–0 with 33 strikeouts in 43 innings. He would win nine of his last eleven decisions, including his last seven, for the longest winning streak on the club. Both he and Leary had 2.91 ERAs for the year.

I was 17–8 after losing a tough one (2–1) in my only outing of the regular season against the Mets on August 24. I had given up just seven hits, and I felt sharp. My stuff was good. Coming off a three-game sweep of the Phillies at Philadelphia and an opening win over the Expos at Montreal, the Dodgers were six-and-a-half games ahead of the league. A victory, our fifth in a row, would set us up nicely for the dog days of September.

All I was concentrating on, going into my next start at Montreal on August 30, was extending our four-game winning streak and trying to distance ourselves from the rest of the pack. I pitched well and felt strong. We jumped ahead early on the Expos. In the second inning with one out, Franklin Stubbs drew a walk and advanced to third on a single to right by John Shelby. After Tracy Woodson lined out to short, Alfredo Griffin singled to right, scoring Stubbs. With Griffin at first and Shelby at second, I doubled to right, scoring both. We were up 3–0.

In the fifth inning, Griffin doubled to right, I sacrificed him to third, and he scored when Steve Sax grounded out to second. I took a 4–0 lead into the bottom of the fifth.

With a man on third and one out, the Expos scored

when Tim Raines doubled to left. Raines scored when Davey Martinez singled to center.

I didn't worry much about the couple of runs the Expos scored in the bottom of the fifth. I held them the rest of the way for a 4–2 victory. I had allowed just six hits, walking two and striking out nine, and I felt good about my third consecutive complete game.

Had I known that those two runs would be the last I would give up during the regular season, or that those final four shutout innings were the start of a streak that would change the record books—not to mention my life—I might have savored the moment. I never gave it a second thought.

12

A SEPTEMBER FOR THE AGES

September can be the most or least fun month of the season, depending on where you are in the standings. While the Braves were out of contention at more than 30 games back, only a dozen or so games separated the first five clubs. We looked forward to a fun, intense, difficult final month of the regular season. Having gone from underdogs to favorites in five months was more than enough for me. There were still those who thought we would fold. They couldn't believe we had made such a turnaround in one season. A lead can evaporate quickly in the last month of the season.

To put into perspective the unbelievable September I had, I need to point out how easy it is to score a run. Realize that a scoreless inning streak does not distinguish between earned and unearned runs. Right there you can see that there are a lot of factors that come into play.

I wouldn't have felt bad if at any point during the streak I had been victimized by an unearned run. It happens. It's not unusual for a pitcher to have 10 percent of the runs scored on him in a season be unearned. Of the 73 runs scored on me in 1988, six were unearned. For some reason, during the streak, errors didn't hurt us. The probabilities of baseball went our way.

But think of all the ways a team can score an *earned* run. Anyone who's been pitching as long as I have has seen his best pitch occasionally rocketed into the stands. Admittedly, a home run is usually hit off of a mistake. A good fastball is too high or covers too much of the heart of the plate. Maybe your sequence of pitches doesn't set up a hitter properly, and thus he's not fooled. You throw a good pitch that's too close to the wheelhouse of a heavy hitter and boom, you've coughed up a run with one swing.

Less frequently, the very pitch you wanted to throw is hit out. I've had hitters seem to be fooled, rock back on their heels, appear to throw the bat at a low, outside, sinking fastball, and hit it for a home run. You'll never see me kick the dirt or fume on the mound after that. My feeling is, *If you can hit that pitch out, you deserve it.* On the other hand, I threw mistakes during the streak and the hitters were either taking, fouled them off, simply didn't hit them well, or hit them *very* well for some loud outs.

What about hits like Texas leaguers, squibs, seeing-eye grounders, bloopers? A pitcher's heart can skip a beat when he sees a hitter like Bobby Bonilla line the hardest-hit ball of the day right at an infielder. Five feet to the other side and that might have been a triple. But then, a routine ground ball might find the hole between third and short. Base hit. Nothing unearned there. Then a blooper falls between two outfielders and an infielder, all running top speed. All three overrun the ball. The man on first was moving with the pitch. He might score. The hitter may wind up on second.

A man on second with no one out can score so many ways it would take another book to outline them all. A slow roller to first puts him on third. With one out, think of the possibilities: sacrifice fly, suicide squeeze, dribbler, you name it. Sometimes even a slow grounder to a pulled-in infield will score a man from third.

Any one of those and hundreds of other things could have scored an innocuous run against us during my streak, and I would simply be a successful pitcher with a good record. I'm not going to pretend that just any pitcher could have had the same luck, but I want to be honest and say that the whole streak could have ended without much noise. The probabilities of baseball took care of the precarious situations when the streak was on the line—especially early, when it was so embryonic that none of us knew where it was leading.

The rest of it I need to share with my teammates. They played magnificently. All the games were close, so even near the end, when I could have been bearing down just to keep the streak alive, I had to bear down for the sake of our pennant drive. It might have been difficult to keep the edge if we had a seven- or eight-run lead by the fifth inning, but we never did.

As I look back on it, there were only a handful of times when an opposing team threatened, because our defense helped keep them off the bases. During the streak I averaged just over five strikeouts per game, not the stuff domination is made of. Luck, good fielding, and good strategy were crucial elements.

What made the month so incredible is that except for the final four innings in the Montreal game—when the whole thing started—it all happened in September. I had six starts, pitched complete game shutouts in the first five then ten scoreless innings in the sixth, had an ERA of 0.00 for the month, won my 20th for the first time in my career, saw my wife give birth to Jordan (our second son) on the 15th, turned 30 the next day, saw us clinch the pennant on the 26th, and broke the consecutive scoreless inning mark on the 28th. Having the playoffs and hopefully the World Series to look forward to in October was too good to be true. Though the streak officially continued into the next regular reason, in my mind it extended into the playoffs because I would face a National League team. Official or not, whatever I added to the streak in the playoffs meant I had gone that many consecutive innings without being scored upon.

Because it's not unusual for any pitcher to close out a game with a few scoreless innings, I certainly wasn't thinking about adding to my four straight innings when I took the mound against the Braves in Atlanta on September 5. I was thinking pennant race. I had been ripped by the Giants, shut out the Expos, lost a heartbreaker to the Mets, and then pitched well in the 4–2 win over the Expos. I wanted to assure myself and my teammates that I was back on track. I had to hit high gear and go after it. We couldn't let the Reds or the Astros catch us.

I hadn't faced the Braves in 1988, but even though they were in last place they still posed a major threat. Dale Murphy, regardless of the type of year he's having, is always dangerous. He had an off year in 1988 and wasn't swinging the bat the way he's capable of swinging it, but he's an outstanding hitter who will wear you out if you make a mistake. Fortunately, we broke out on top 2–0 in the first half of the first inning on singles by Alfredo Griffin and Mickey Hatcher, an error, a hit batsman, and a walk.

Atlanta threatened in the bottom half when Gerald Perry, their hard-hitting first baseman, hit a double to left off me with two out. Had I been worried about a streak, I might have been more careful pitching to Murphy after that. He ran the count to 3–2, then I struck him out for the first of four straight times that night. We scored only once more, but we already had all we needed. After giving up no-out singles in each of the next two innings, I was saved by a double play in the second and good fielding in the third, so no one got past second base. I found my rhythm after that and pitched five perfect innings. Until I gave up a leadoff single in the ninth, I had retired 16 straight hitters, five on strikes. I finished the game with a record of 19–8, having given up four hits, allowing one walk, and striking out eight.

We lost three of our next four games and fell to just four games ahead of Houston. When I took the mound against the Reds at Dodger Stadium on September 10, we needed a victory, badly. For one thing, the Reds had won eight of their last 10 and 11 of their last 16 and had slipped into third place, five and a half games behind us and a game and a half behind Houston. Their ace, Danny Jackson, had beat us the night before for his 21st victory of the season and was everybody's early favorite for the Cy Young award. One writer said he had a "virtual lock" on the award, and Reds manager Pete Rose pointed out that Danny had more wins, fewer losses, more complete games, and more shutouts than I did.

My original goal for the season had been to make the All-Star Team for the second straight year. When I did that and had 13 wins by the break, I set my sights on 20 wins for the season. It's not that big of a deal, because a pretty fair pitcher on a great team can win 20 without being as impressive as a guy who might be 14–11 or so on a club in last place. But 19–3 was the best I had ever done, so 20 would be nice. More important, of course, was beating the Reds and keeping them in third place. That's why when I faced Eric Davis with two outs and the bases loaded in the third inning, I was just trying to keep him in the park. He had already hit 25 dingers in 1988, and he led the league in game-winning RBIs with 16.

We hadn't scored yet, and I figured a single would mean only two runs. I couldn't let Davis hit one out. He was called out on a checked third strike. His next two times up he hit into a pair of double plays. In the top of the seventh, with one out and runners on first and third, I got Ken Griffey to pop out, and then I struck out Barry Larkin.

By then we were leading 3–0, and Demper, our reserve catcher behind Sosh, hit a two-run insurance homer in the bottom of the eighth to ice it. I had to be a little lucky to beat the Reds, because they usually hit me like they knew what was coming. It's not easy to scatter seven hits and still get a shutout, especially when you walk three. But with eight strikeouts and two double plays, things worked out.

Our five runs would prove to be the biggest margin of any of the games in the streak. I was starting to get into it, bearing down on every pitch, animated on the mound, scolding myself for mistakes, pumping up myself and others as we kept succeeding. It was still too early to be thinking streak, though reporters began mentioning that I hadn't been scored on in 22 innings. I couldn't tell if this was the best I'd ever pitched, but I knew every pitch seemed like my last. I concentrated and bore down on every one. I figured I had four starts left. I wanted to win them all to help assure us of the title.

Tommy Lasorda was especially flattering after the game. He said the mantle had fallen to me to be the stopper in 1988. Demper told reporters he put me in Jim Palmer's category as the type of pitcher who can carry a team. He said, "A lot of pitchers go out there afraid to lose. But then there are those like Orel who aren't afraid to go out there and do what they want. It's fun to catch a guy like that."

The next night we had another great finish. Jeff Hamilton homered in the bottom of the ninth to beat Cincinnati 5–3. By the time I started again on September 14 at home against Atlanta, we had won four straight. John Tudor had shut out the Braves the night before and began an amazing streak for Dodger pitchers. In seven games we would win six, including five shutouts. Our only loss in that string would be 1-0 to Cincinnati, despite a three-hit, seven-strikeout performance by Tim Belcher. He would lose the toughest way possible. His opponent, Tom Browning, threw a perfect game. Belcher came back after that disappointment to pitch the last shutout in the chain. We would win nine of ten and in our last seven games allow just four runs.

I had two more shutouts during that incredible week, both 1–0 nail-biters. The first came September 14 against Atlanta at home. I pitched on three days' rest because Tommy and Perry wanted to set me up to pitch against Houston after a series in Cincinnati. That worked out well for Jamie and me, because we expected our baby the next morning. Since I wasn't scheduled to pitch against the Reds anyway, I would be able to stay in California one day while the rest of the team went to Cincy. That way I could be at the hospital with Jamie.

I was going fine against the Braves into the top of the seventh when Andres Thomas led off with a double to the gap in left-center. Dion James grounded to first, but Franklin Stubbs's throw pulled me off the bag and Thomas went to third.

Ozzie Virgil, always a potential menace, grounded to Stubbs, who made the putout himself and held Thomas at third, James advancing to second. With first base open and only one out, I pitched carefully to Jerry Blocker, going to 2–0 before intentionally walking him to load the bases and face the pitcher, Rick Mahler. I struck him out but then had to face Ron Gant. I threw a curve, and as soon as it left my hand I shouted, "No!" I had hung it. Gant lifted a long fly ball to left, and I held my breath. Gibson crashed into the wall but hauled it in, and I was out of my third jam in the game.

Meanwhile, Mahler was pitching an outstanding game for Atlanta, allowing just five hits and walking only two. We went into the bottom of the ninth in a scoreless tie. We needed the top of our order to get on so hitters like Gibson and Marshall could drive them in, but it hadn't been happening all game. So Gibson worked a walk to lead off the ninth, and Marshall knew he'd probably get a fastball with a baserunning threat at first. Moose got the heater and hammered it into the corner in left for a double, and Gibson never slowed till he crossed the plate. "No one was going to stop me," he said.

Just before the game-winning hit I told Tommy I was ready to pitch the tenth inning, if necessary. "Oh, no you're not," he told me. "Not on three days' rest, you're not. I'm not gonna take the chance of your gettin' hurt." Since the only place I was going the next day was the maternity ward, I really wanted to continue. I was sure glad I didn't have to. I think Tommy assumed I was just begging to play more, like I always do, even bugging him to let me relieve when I feel good.

Now the streak was beginning to look interesting to the writers, but ironically it was still short of the 33⅔ straight scoreless innings I had pitched as a newcomer to the starting rotation on 1984. I don't recall anyone back then predicting a challenge to Don Drysdale's 1968 mark of 58⅔ innings. His mark was considered as unreachable as Joe DiMaggio's 56-game hitting streak.

I still considered Drysdale's mark untouchable, and I said so. The record was slightly more than 27 innings away, and I wondered if I had that much strength left in my arm. Even if the impossible happened and I pitched three more consecutive nine-inning shutouts, I would still need a relief

BEN HINES 35

September, 1988, is quite a month for me. By the 26th, I'm in the middle of a scoreless inning streak, have become a 20-game winner for the first time in my career, have become a father again, and have turned 30. That day we prove the pre-season experts wrong by clinching the Western Division Championship in San Diego.

The scoreboard tells the story in San Diego. Those 10 shutout innings put me over the top, giving me 59 straight and breaking Don Drysdale's 20-year-old record.

What a thrill to be interviewed by Dodger broadcaster Don Drysdale, whose record I have just broken.

At a ceremony in honor of the streak, I protect newborn Jordan from the sun while manager Tommy Lasorda salutes Jamie by presenting her with a 59-pearl necklace—one for each scoreless inning.

(below)

Eight more consecutive shutout innings—against the Mets in the first game of the National League Championship Series (NLCS)—do not count as part of the streak because they come in post-season play. I finally allow a run in the ninth, and the Mets come back to beat us 3-2.

I look on helplessly after being removed in the ninth. Despite good relief pitching, the breaks all go the Mets' way.

Even with long underwear, I'm freezing. But this is the NLCS and I don't allow myself to even think about it.

The New York ground crew has major work to do between almost every inning of game three in the NLCS. The game has been postponed a day due to rain and, had it not been a post-season game, probably would have been delayed again due to cold, drizzle, and field conditions.

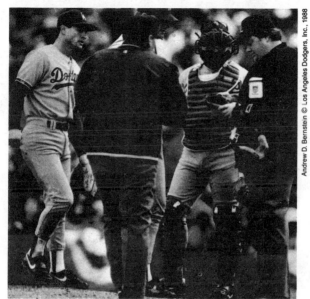

The most controversial point in the playoffs comes in game three, when Jay Howell, in relief for me, is ejected when the umpires find pine tar on his glove.

Game four, ninth inning, bases loaded, two outs. Mets fans on their feet, and Kevin McReynolds at the plate—I volunteer to relieve after pitching seven innings the night before. Steve Sax, Rick Dempsey, and Ron Perranoski welcome me to the mound.

Mets fans welcome me in their own way.

One of the most exciting and dramatic times I ever experience on the mound. Three pitches later the league series is tied at two games apiece.

Every pitcher loves to hit. Here I line one to left in game seven of the NLCS against the Mets.

Tommy, the cheerleader, greets me between innings. My game face is well fixed.

In the first game of the World Series, Kirk Gibson provides one of the greatest finishes and most dramatic moments I've ever seen in baseball.

Andrew D. Bernstein © Los Angeles Dodgers, Inc., 1988

You never want to show up the other team, but I can't hide a smile after getting Jose Canseco and Dave Parker to end the Oakland threat in the eighth inning of the final game of the World Series.

"Hershiser looking to the skies and singing for inspiration may have been my favorite sports scene of the year." — Rick Telander, *Sports Illustrated*

Even though the Dodgers have been celebrating on the field, it still doesn't hit me until I catch Jamie's eye in the crowd. Across a sea of faces we "connect" and I'm finally able to let the grin come. We have done it. We have won the World Series!

The World Championship Trophy is now ours.

appearance or some fluke to add another inning and break the record in 1988.

I told reporters, "I see Don's record as one that won't be broken. I don't see it happening."

Did I think about it privately? Sure, mentioning it only to Jamie. We thought about how incredible it would be, but it wasn't a frequent topic of conversation. It was just too far away. I was barely over halfway there at 31 innings. While I may have let the possibility dance in my head, I was honest when I said I didn't see it. In fact, we laughed at the thought.

The next day, September 15, Jamie gave birth to Jordan. We were thrilled, but there were immediate complications. With fluid in his lungs he was placed in intensive care. We were devastated. I called friends and family and asked them to pray. Everything else in my life paled as father-love washed over me. I stood helplessly by Jordan's incubator and watched his tiny heart race and his lungs gasp for air. Tubes and wires engulfed his frail body. They took blood from his heel and fed him intravenously.

The next day, my thirtieth birthday, slid by without a thought. By radio I followed one of the rarest events in major league baseball: Tom Browning throwing his perfect game against us. It didn't matter. The only thing that mattered was Jordan. Happy birthday, Orel.

13

A SEPTEMBER FOR THE AGES II

I called Tommy Lasorda in Cincinnati. "I think I need to stay as long as possible here with Jamie and the baby. I know I'm missing my workouts, but I'll work out here."

Tommy, a family man through and through, wouldn't have it any other way. "Bulldog, you know what's best. I know you'll be ready to pitch. You've always been ready before. Do what you need to do." That might seem like the only logical response an employer could have, but don't forget I was being paid $1.1 million to be at my best whenever they needed me. I wanted to get to Cincinnati as soon as possible, but I wouldn't leave until Jordan was better. As it developed, he didn't pull out of danger until the day before I was to pitch in Houston. I flew directly there, deciding on the plane that in spite of it all, I owed it to the Dodgers to give my full attention to the game.

I remembered that four years before, when Quinton was just learning to crawl, he had fallen off a bed and broken his collarbone. Needless to say, that had weighed heavily on my mind when I pitched in San Diego against the Padres that night. In the first inning I had given up two quick hits and a walk, and suddenly I had bases loaded and nobody out.

"Wait a minute, dummy," I had scolded myself, "you can't be thinking about Quinton. Either pitch this game or get off the mound and go home and be with him."

The fact was, I would be with Quinton soon enough. He was fine in Jamie's care, and it wasn't like I was a callous father who thought his game or his profession was more important than his son. It was just that I had a job to do. I needed to set aside my emotions for a couple of hours, or I would be doing a disservice to my teammates. I pitched out of the jam, giving up only one run, and went on to win 3–1.

After that game the first question from reporters was not about the game but, "How's Quinton?" I burst into tears and had to walk away for a few minutes. You can set aside you feelings only for so long, especially when it comes to tenderness for a child. So, four years later, in the middle of a pennant race and a scoreless inning streak, and making more than four times the money I had in 1984, I knew what it was going to take to pitch against the Astros with little Jordan having just been moved from intensive to intermediate care. I had satisfied myself that there was nothing more I could do for him and Jamie there, and she encouraged me to go and do my best.

I foresaw that everyone on the club would wish me luck and ask me how Jordan was. All that would do was keep my mind focused on my baby, and I would be good for nothing on the mound. I had to make the decision again to postpone my fatherly compassion, to relegate that to the off-the-mound Orel. On the mound I couldn't be that other person. I wasn't paid to be a husband and father; I was paid to be the hitter's worst nightmare, a pitcher who keeps coming at you.

I reminded myself that the best thing I could do for Jordan was to pitch my best, then call home and check in on him and Jamie. Nothing would be served by dwelling on the problem. If my mind was in Los Angeles, my pitches would wind up in the seats.

At the pre-game team meeting on September 19, I told the guys, "I'm glad to be back. I want you to know Jordan's okay, and I just want to concentrate on beating these guys." That eliminated the need for anyone to ask about him and to get that emotion welling up inside me when I couldn't do anything about it. I pitched one of my best games during the streak, allowing just four singles, two of them to Kevin Bass, and no walks. In the first inning Bass singled with two outs, stole second, and reached third on an error. Fortunately, I got Buddy Bell to fly out.

John Shelby hit a seventh inning solo homer to right for our only run, and I had recorded my fourth straight shutout and seventh straight complete game. The way our offense was going, our pitching staff had to be in a shutout mode to keep winning. Our team batting average for the month to that point was a ridiculous .189, yet we enjoyed our biggest lead in the standings, and our magic number to clinch the pennant dropped to five. We could have been worried about the offense, but we knew it would come around, and we hoped it would be in time for the playoffs.

The press still had me competing with Danny Jackson of the Reds for the Cy Young award. Gerald Young of the Astros said I should win it. "He couldn't walk the ball up to the plate any better. Very rarely do you find a pitch he doesn't put exactly where he wants. Definitely the best in the league."

The scoreless inning string reached 40 now, and the press was lit up about it. I still saw it as a long, long shot, especially given that I would need 19 more full scoreless innings, and I had just two starts left. Even if I pitched two more shutouts, which looked like Mount Everest at the time, I would fall an inning short.

Don Drysdale, now a Dodger broadcaster, began to be quoted about the chase. He was totally in my corner, saying records were made to be broken. "I'm just glad it's another Dodger with a uniform number in the fifties (Drysdale wore number 53; I wear 55). You can tell what they think of you as a rookie when they give you those football numbers. Nobody expects you to make the team. Orel and I have that in common."

The problem was, I needed 57 more outs without a run to break the record. It was too much to think about. I was only two-thirds of the way there. I was happy enough with what I had accomplished already. First, of course, was the success of the Dodgers. I wanted the pennant more than any personal record (my 22 victories were already the most in one season by a Dodger since Koufax had won 27 in

1966). With his 58⅔ consecutive scoreless innings in 1968, Drysdale had broken Walter Johnson's 1916 record of 55⅔. Later in 1968 Bob Gibson had 47. Carl Hubbell recorded 45⅓ in 1933. One more shutout would push me past both Hubbell and Gibson.

So, even though I had to admit that the record was quite a dream, I didn't expect it or predict it. I lay in bed in the hotel in Houston that night and talked to Jamie on the phone, getting the good news on Jordan's improvement.

Before we hung up, I said, "Wouldn't it be neat to actually get into a game where tying the record was within reach?" Still we just laughed about it. I confess I wanted to get at least one more shutout so I would be within "striking" distance. If I got that close I wouldn't be thrilled about not making it, but just being in that situation would have been exciting.

My next start was September 23 at Candlestick Park in San Francisco, a tough park to pitch in. The crowd is close and loud, and the Giants play well at home. Strange things happen at that ballpark. And strange things happen against the Giants. I felt I owed them something for the five earned runs I gave up in just two innings the last time I faced them.

Twenty years before, on May 31, 1968, Drysdale was going after his fifth straight shutout on the way to the record. The Dodgers were leading the Giants 3–0 in the top of the ninth at home when Drysdale loaded the bases with no one out. It appeared only a miracle could keep his streak alive in its 45th inning. Then came the miracle. With Dick Dietz batting and a 2–2 count, Drysdale hit him with a pitch. End of shutout, end of streak. But plate umpire Harry Wendelstedt ruled that Dietz had made no effort to get out of the way. The pitch was called a ball, and somehow Drysdale got Dietz and the next two hitters out.

Now, against the Giants, I'm in trouble in the third inning, the 43rd of the streak. Jose Uribe leads off with a single, and pitcher Atlee Hammaker tries to sacrifice him to second. I slip trying to get to the ball, and both runners are safe. Brett Butler then pushes a groundball to third where Jeff Hamilton elects to go for the double play, second to first. Hammaker is forced at second, Uribe stopped at third, but Butler beats the relay to first. Now I've got men at first and third and only one out, and Ernest Riles is at the plate.

A fly ball will score a run. A hit, an error, a wild pitch will all score a run. I need a double play grounder, so I'm pumping the sinker in there as hard as I can. Success. Riles hits a bouncer to Sax at second, who tosses to Griffin covering. I hold my breath. Griffin's throw to first sails wide and the run scores. I grimace and let out a huge breath. It's disappointing to come so close and a real letdown to see it all end, but now we're trailing 1–0 and I have to face Will Clark.

I was rubbing up the ball and turning back toward the mound when I saw second base umpire Paul Range signal that both Butler and Riles were out. I headed straight for the dugout before he changed his mind. I knew exactly what he was saying. Butler had apparently slid outside the baseline at Griffin and was called for interference. Both runners are automatically out, the run doesn't count, the streak stays alive, as does the shutout. When I got to the dugout both Tommy and Perry were laughing. "Drysdale got his break," Tommy said. "Now you got yours!"

"Dietz revisited," I said.

"When you're hot, you're hot!"

I was hot the rest of the way, retiring the next nine hitters in a row. Though I struck out only two, I allowed just lone singles in the seventh and eighth after that. I pitched carefully to Will Clark throughout the game, worried about the wind blowing out to right and not wanting to give him anything to hit out. I didn't care if he got a hit; I just didn't want him breaking up the game—or the streak—with one swing. He went one for three with a single.

In the top of the eighth Mickey Hatcher hit a three-run homer, his first in 172 at-bats in the season, and that was all we needed. The streak was at 49 innings, and the media had gone crazy. I admitted that the record may be more attainable now than it had been, but to get another shutout would be unbelievable. "I'd have to pitch ten innings in my last start anyway. To say the record is breakable is crazy."

Even if I pitched another shutout, I would finish the season two-thirds of an inning short of the record. The statistics people said Drysdale's record should be seen as 58 innings even, but everyone would know I had fallen short. I knew the streak could continue into the next baseball season, but extending a streak after six months' rest is one thing, breaking it is another. After all this, even another shutout supposedly would result in a tied record (actually a little short) and an asterisk.

"I just want to put up as many zeroes as I can," I told the press. "Our magic number is two and my streak seems to coincide with what the team has done."

I had done what I had hoped. I was within reaching a technical tie in one game. I had passed Carl Hubbell and Bob Gibson, and now only Walter Johnson and Don Drysdale were ahead of me. My five consecutive shutouts put me in a category with only two other pitchers in history (Drysdale had six in 1968, and Doc White had five in 1904). The win was my 23rd, my sixth in a row, and a club record-tying eighth straight complete game.

Don Drysdale was more encouraging than ever. He told people, "Orel's pitching well and he's in a great frame of mind. He's such a great kid that I'm having fun watching him. I'm happy for him, and I'm glad I'm around to see him do this." Jim Murray, the syndicated sports columnist with the *Los Angeles Times*, wrote: "Five shutouts in a season is Cy Young stuff. Five shutouts in a row is Hall of Fame stuff."

Three games later, on Monday night, September 26, the Dodgers clinched the National League's Western Division pennant with a 3–2 victory over the San Diego Padres. Mickey Hatcher got the game-winning hit, and suddenly the Stuntman who had been having trouble at the plate was coming around just in time to help us.

Jay Howell got the save, giving our bullpen a club record 47 for the season. We had turned our won-loss record around from two straight 73–89 years to 92–64 with five games to go. In a week we would host the New York Mets for the first two games of the National League Championship Series. The only question left for the regular season was what would happen to my streak. It stood at five shutouts after four scoreless innings for 49. I would start two nights later against these same Padres at Jack Murphy Stadium in San Diego.

I couldn't believe it was happening. Still happening. When I was four and then three shutouts away from the record, I think no one really believed it would get this far. Tommy Lasorda admits he thought no one would ever approach Drysdale's record. But now it was 9⅔ innings away. I had been living a charmed life for a month, not allowing a run since August 30. I wouldn't have even wanted to know the odds against one more shutout.

14

THE BIG NIGHT

It had actually been good for me that we didn't clinch the pennant earlier, because then the pressure would have been off. Every pitch wouldn't have meant as much. Now that I was this close, I could bear down like it was the last game of the World Series, but if I had needed three or four more shutouts when the wins didn't mean anything, I doubt I could have done it. Going into the seventh inning in each of the three previous games, we were engaged in scoreless ties. We had scored all of 13 runs during the streak so far.

Now I hoped that if I got a man on third with no one out maybe Tommy would pull in the infield to keep the run from scoring on a routine ground ball, something a defense normally wouldn't do early in a ball game.

My career record against the Padres was 7–4, including four shutouts, a one-hitter, a two-hitter, and a 1.90 ERA. In my only previous appearance against the Padres in 1988, I had allowed two runs on seven hits in a 12–2 complete game victory.

One of the toughest things about this game would be the prospect of facing Tony Gwynn, probably the best hitter in the National League. He was a two-time league batting champion and was on his way to a third. Tony always seems to get wood on the ball, and he usually drives it with authority. I try to keep the ball away from him. I don't even dream of trying to strike him out. He hits me as well as anyone in the National League.

Tony and I love to battle each other. I've been called a thinking pitcher; well, he's a thinking man's hitter. He watches the video tapes, memorizes sequences of pitches, and is the last guy you want to see come up with a man on third and less than two outs. He will get the bat on the ball. He'll score that runner somehow. I suggested to him before the game that he might want to take the night off.

Tony had some nice things to say about me to the press: "Orel's awesome, simple as that. He throws any pitch he wants, anywhere he wants, any time in the count, always for a strike. He never gives in. If he falls behind, he's as likely to throw a change-up as a fastball. Whatever you least expect, that's what he'll do." Padres' pitcher Mark Grant said I couldn't place my pitches any better if I used a tee.

The question I got most before the game was what would happen if I pitched a shutout. Would I pitch an inning of relief before the end of the season to try to break the record? I was sure Tommy would give me that chance, but the question was so premature! It assumed a shutout, a sixth in a row. What to do after that seemed a luxury to have to worry about in advance. In fact, however, I *had* considered it. This is what I wanted to do, if I had a choice: Make a relief appearance at Dodger Stadium before the home crowd, but not break the record. Get two outs, tie it, and leave the mound with Don Drysdale and me at the top of the heap. It would be a slap in his face to break the record in a relief appearance. Was I nuts not to want to break the record? I didn't think so. I honestly couldn't see myself in Don's category. He was a Hall of Fame pitcher. At the Dodger spring training facility in Vero Beach, Florida, there's even a room named after Don in honor of his streak! He was great. I was just one of the guys. I was nine years old when he set the record in 1968.

The afternoon before the game I had lunch with Tim Belcher, who told me later he was determined not to bring up any talk of the record. In an attempt to keep me occupied and off the subject, he handed me a copy of that morning's *USA Today*. He hadn't looked at it. "Hey, Timmy, look at this," I said, unfolding the front page for him. There were big pictures of Drysdale and me in a major feature on the record.

Don himself admitted he was superstitious enough not to want to talk to me about the record or do anything that would jinx me. When he interviewed me after we clinched the division, he didn't say a word about the scoreless streak. I wasn't superstitious, but I did not want to choke. I wanted to at least get to the point in the game where I could experience that excitement, that feeling of going after a no-hitter, a perfect game, something special, where there's electricity in the air and everyone in the stands knows exactly what the stakes are. That way, even if I fell short, I would have had the opportunity to experience that feeling. There's nothing like it.

* * *

I mechanically worked my way through all my normal road trip pre-game preparations, telling myself over and over to treat this like any other game. I had to focus on mechanics, concentrate on release points, not remind myself how many innings or outs were needed to tie the record.

I was glad when it was time to head for the bullpen and start throwing with Perry watching. I threw a few pitches and turned to him. "You know, I'm really pretty nervous. I can even feel it in my stomach."

"You'll be all right once you get out there and get the first couple of outs," Perry said.

I continued to throw.

"Did you hear that?" he said suddenly.

"No."

"That was *my* stomach. I think I'm nervous too!"

When I was warming up on the mound before the bottom of the first inning, I was razzed by San Diego fans. "You've been lucky, Hershiser! We're not only gonna score off you, we're gonna kill you!" All that did was pump me up.

In the Padre dugout the players encouraged each other. "Let's jump on this guy early! Start it right now. Get it over quick." It reminded me how excited the Giants' bench had been when they thought they had scored on me and broken the string. But I was hardly challenged early. Neither was the Padre starter, Andy Hawkins. Every time Tony Gwynn came to the plate I kept the ball away from him. He and Carmelo Martinez hit the hardest shots all night, both foul. Tony grounded out to second four times.

My case of nerves turned to excitement by the fourth inning when both Hawkins and I were breezing along unscored upon. The fans continued to rag on me between innings until we got deep into the game and the record appeared to be within sight. Then I heard more positive comments. Through six innings, I had thrown 65 pitches, 45 of them strikes, and allowed just two hits. I got to a three-ball count only twice. When we went into the seventh, for the fourth game in a row I was pitching in a scoreless ball game. On my way out of the dugout I got a standing ovation. Talk about a rush! These were Padre fans who really knew what was going on. They cheered every out. They cheered me on my way back to the dugout and up to the plate. The last out in the seventh gave me 56 innings and pushed me past Walter Johnson's 55⅔.

With two out in the eighth, Roberto Alomar singled, and the crowd came alive. He's a real base-stealing threat, but I was determined not to let him get into scoring position. No Padre had made it past first all night, so I decided I would throw to first base until Alomar got tired of leading off so far. I may not have wanted to break Dysdale's record, but I certainly didn't want to miss tying it. With a 1–0 count on Tim Flannery, I caught Alomar leaning the wrong way and picked him off. The record stood at 57 innings.

There had been a lot of controversy about the record being 58 or 58⅔ innings, because some people said a fraction of a scoreless inning does not constitute a scoreless inning. Otherwise, you have to count the last out of the last inning someone scored against you as ⅓ inning. I knew that if I shut out the Padres in the bottom of the ninth, some experts would say I had tied Drysdale. But everyone knew he had gone two more outs before allowing a run, so to me, that was what I needed to do to tie him.

I couldn't believe my luck, first that I had again gone this long in a game without giving up a run, but more astounding, that the Dodgers had not scored either, making that extra inning look like a possibility. Even though we had already clinched the pennant, however, I was not hoping we would remain scoreless into the tenth. I like to win. I wanted my 24th victory. I didn't expect to pitch more than two outs in the tenth anyway, if we made it that far.

In the top of the ninth, while Sosh was taking off his catching gear and getting ready to hit, he asked me, "Do you want me to hit one out, or just a base hit so you can have a chance at the record?" That from a slugger with all of three home runs for the season! It was the first time anyone on the team talked to me the whole night. Sosh neither hammered nor got a base hit, and we didn't score.

The bottom of the ninth was easier than I deserved, three ground ball outs. Tommy was the first to greet me as I came off the field, and it was time to talk. I had thrown only 98 pitches so far. "Let me tie it at home," I said. He rolled his eyes and beckoned Perry and Ben Hines, our batting coach. "You hear this guy? No way! You're goin' out there, Bulldog! You owe it to yourself and to the team. And to baseball."

"Then let me just tie it and leave it there."

"No. I'm not takin' you out. You're gonna pitch, and I want three outs."

The other two nodded. It was unanimous. I had been serious and sincere, but I was also an employee, a player. I did what managers and coaches said.

The Dodgers didn't score in the top of the inning, giving me my tenth straight inning and one chance to legitimately break the record, all in the same season. It was too good to be true. If someone had made up a story like this, it would never sell. I went to the mound and scanned the park for Drysdale. I didn't see him in the press box. I didn't see him on the field. He must have been on his way to the dugout, because I found out later that it was from there that he watched the last inning. I gave up searching for him but, hoping he could see me, I tipped my cap toward the press box. "I'm going for it, Don," I whispered. And I went for it.

I struck Marvelle Wynne out to lead off the tenth, but the pitch got away from me and bounced past Sosh. Wynne wound up at first, so even after a strikeout (only my second of the game), I still needed three outs. That was a bad sign.

Benito Santiago, whose rookie streak of 34 games I had ironically broken up the year before, sacrificed Wynne to second, and now I was in trouble. Randy Ready grounded to short, sending Wynne to third with two outs. Don Drysdale and I stood alone at the top of the heap, and I felt inadequate. I would have voluntarily tied him by walking off the mound, but that idea had been rejected, and there was no way I was going to intentionally let a run score.

So it had come to this: a run 90 feet away, with Garry Templeton at the plate. We decided we could use a runner at first to set up a force at second. The winning run was at third anyway, so Templeton would be a meaningless runner except for the advantage it gave us. I would much rather face the pitcher or his pinch hitter in that situation, so we decided to intentionally walk Templeton. It would be my only walk of the game.

After the second pitch of the unintentional walk, I casually strode away from Sosh's return throw and had to desperately lunge back to keep the ball from going into centerfield. I caught it in the web of my glove and smiled wryly at Wynne on third. He smiled back. What a way for the streak to have ended! I would have had no one to blame but myself.

Hawkins was supposed to be the next hitter, but though he had matched me with a ten-inning, four-hit shutout, the Padres had to play the percentages and go for the run. It wasn't just the streak they were trying to derail. A run for them now meant the ball game, too. Keith Moreland was sent in to pinch hit.

I'd had luck with Moreland in the past. His career average against me was less than .200. I thought he was susceptible to a low, outside curveball, but I didn't dare try it for fear of a wild pitch or a passed ball. I would have never forgiven myself. I got two quick called strikes on him, and the crowd was standing, cheering every pitch. Then he fouled one off. I gave him a fastball, up and away, and he went after it, lifting a high, shallow fly ball to right field. Jose Gonzalez gathered it in. I stood with my hands on my knees, staring out there. I couldn't hide my grin. It was over. The pressure was off. I could start thinking about the Mets.

But not yet. My teammates on the field and from the bench mobbed me, and Don Drysdale met me at the end of the dugout. We embraced. "It couldn't have happened to a nicer kid," he said with a smile. "I can't believe you didn't win that game—just like the sixties." He interviewed me right there for KABC radio while the game was still going on. I told him my plan had been just to tie the record. He scowled at me. "If I'd known that I'd have kicked you in the rear and told you to get your buns out there and go for it."

Even though I had retired 19 Padres on ground balls and was probably as sharp as I had been all year, I would not get a decision in the game. It would not count as a shutout or a complete game, even though it really was more impressive than either of those. During the streak I had allowed 30 hits, struck out 33, and walked eight.

I was getting my arm iced when Mike Williams, our public relations director, told me I was wanted at a press conference. "During the game!?" He nodded. More than fifty reporters crowded around, wanting to talk to me and to Drysdale. After a few minutes he told them, "It's his night. Listen to him now."

I said I hoped we'd win the game. (We would lose 2–1 on a pinch hit homer, despite scoring the first run of the game in the top of the sixteenth.) The streak had been a dream, but I was glad it was over for 1988. All those innings wouldn't mean a thing when Mookie Wilson came to the plate for the Mets in the first game of the National League Championship Series.

We would be one of the biggest underdogs in the history of post-season play. Despite our turnaround, most experts felt we didn't even belong in the playoffs.

15

ANTICIPATION

I was naive to think I could put the streak behind me. The pressure was off as far as tying or breaking it, of course, and though it would continue the next regular season, no one would let it die. As for me, I consider the record Drysdale's until I retire. Whose record is it? It's not mine. I broke his. For as long as I pitch, I will be known as the guy who broke Drysdale's record. When I'm gone from the game, the record will be mine.

During the pre-playoff hoopla, I was being considered a shoo-in for the Cy Young award and was also the center of a controversy about overwork. The thinking went like this: if pitching is all the Dodgers have, and Hershiser is their ace, they'll be hopeless against the Mets after he pitched eight consecutive complete games and then went ten innings.

I skipped the last home series and had plenty of rest, and anyway I believed it was good mechanics that not only allowed me to pitch so well for so long, but which also protected my arm. If I had done all that pressure pitching with just a strong arm, it would have been jelly by the end of the season.

Our secret, however, was that we had several other fine pitchers with good stuff and records to prove it. Belcher and Leary had had good years, Tudor proved a fine addition, and our bullpen was outstanding. As a staff, the Dodgers were second in the league in wins, second in ERAs, first in complete games, first in shutouts, first in saves, and second in least runs, earned runs, and home runs allowed. Our bullpen was first in the league with a 2.35 ERA and 47 saves, and tied for first in wins (27).

The Dodgers seemed weak offensively because we had to scratch for so many victories. Gibby had been hobbled with leg injuries, and Mike Marshall was also sidelined occasionally. Our hope was, of course, that they would return to top form for the playoffs. We finished sixth in the league in hitting, despite the fact that Gibby, Sax, and Marshall finished high in several individual categories. That made us look suspect, however, because the division winner usually finishes higher than sixth in hitting.

As a team we had our best road record (49–31) since 1974, which led the National League and was second in the big leagues only to Oakland (50–31).

What I liked best about our chances, though, had more to do with the spirit on our team. We cared about each other. We were all gung-ho. Everybody hustled, everybody tried, nobody would give up until the last out was recorded. We believed in ourselves and in each other. It wasn't phony. It wasn't sentimental. We had set out to do a job and to accomplish a goal, and we all knew there were no shortcuts.

Any doubts I had about how I was accepted on the club were dispelled when I saw how the guys responded when I broke the record. I told Jamie, "They were honestly happy for me." That was important to me. I know I've had the reputation of a guy who thinks he can do anything—start, relieve, hit, coach, whatever—and I may get on people's nerves when I keep bugging the coaches to let me relieve, but the genuine affection and sincere congratulations I received from everybody set my mind at ease. If they had any doubts about my character or wondered whether I was just trying to be a coach's pet rather than a hardworking, teachable professional, I hope those doubts were dispelled by my performance.

The key now was not to rest on my laurels. How could a person ask for a better season's end than I had just had? Had we dropped four straight to the Mets and had I had a couple of fair outings, I wouldn't have had to hang my head. But I don't play to be satisfactory. Our job had just begun. The division pennant means little if you go on to lose the league championship and don't get to play in the World Series. And just getting to the Series is acceptable only to teams who have never been there before. Don't believe all those quotes about how good it is to "just be here" and that "that's the important thing."

The most important thing is doing the right thing the right way and letting the results take care of themselves, but the whole point, the purpose of baseball, is to win. If you do your best and lose, hold your head high, but don't tell me just getting to the Series is all that matters. We wanted it all. We wanted to beat the Mets, certainly the most talented team in the National League, and then we wanted to beat the Red Sox or the Athletics for the world championship. The world wouldn't come to an end if we failed, but success was what we were after.

We knew full well we were considered the weakest of the four teams left in the big leagues. It was assumed, because we had lost 10 of 11 to the Mets during the regular season, that they would quickly dispose of us and then face probably the monstrous-hitting Athletics. We had to remind ourselves that the 1983 Dodgers beat the Phillies 11 times in 12 games during the regular season, then lost to them in the playoffs.

The 1988 Dodgers were injury-riddled, besides being talent-poor (so "they" said), so we were the only ones who thought we had a chance. And we weren't just whistling in the dark. If we won the championship and the Series, everyone but us would be surprised. You don't win the National League West on a fluke, especially when you play over 160 games. Unless our division was the weak sister of the four in the majors—and we didn't believe that for a minute—we were going into the post-season with as good a shot as anyone.

Sure, having lost 10 of 11 to the Mets gave us something to think about. But to give you an idea of our mind-set, we reminded each other that those losses had not cost us our pennant and that they didn't count in the playoffs. We would start even with the Mets, at home. If they won four before we did, fine, they could take the trophy into the World Series. But they were going to have to do it on the field and not in the newspapers. We weren't conceding anything.

Oddsmakers and reporters had us in the grave already because of injuries, and they *were* troubling.

Fernando Valenzuela was scratched from the lineup because his shoulder had not come around. He had pitched seven innings after coming off the disabled list and had allowed only one earned run. But he was not sharp. He wasn't ready, and he and everyone else knew it. It had to be hard for him to ride the bench and watch when he had been the heart and soul of our pitching staff for years. He'll be back.

Dave Anderson had back troubles and was replaced by Mike Sharperson. John Tudor's hip bothered him, and he was moved back in the rotation. I was to start the first game against Dwight Gooden. Rookie Tim Belcher would start game two against hard-throwing David Cone. Tudor would then start game three for us. Worse for us was that Kirk Gibson's chronic hamstring behind his left knee was flaring up. No one could tell how effective he would be, though he would start in game one. (Our team physician is Dr. Frank Jobe, and a local sportswriter started calling the Dodger wounded "the patients of Jobe.")

All this was wonderful for Tommy. Of course, he never likes to see anyone injured, but he's best at managing a team where managerial savvy is really needed. Regardless of what the media was saying, a healthy Dodger team is a great club that can be counted on to go out and win ball games. But when you have to patch together a starting lineup with minor leaguers, rookies, and reserves, managerial strategy becomes as important as the talent on the field. Tommy would be in his element, making things happen, conniving, inspiring, jiving, hustling. He would, somehow, will this team to win no matter who comprised the lineup.

I felt good about the opener because I didn't have the pressure of keeping a scoreless streak alive. I never want to be scored on, but in a seven-game playoff the important thing is to keep your offense in the game. You might give up a run to keep from giving up more in some situations. In my mind, because we were playing the Mets, any scoreless innings I pitched would extend my streak. Even if it wasn't official, it would be actual. I could say I threw that many in a row against legitimate competition in my own league during the same season, with no rest, and without taking advantage of a club from another league who hadn't seen me before.

But that was the extent of my thinking about pitching shutouts. The important thing was to beat the Mets, get an early lead in the championship series, and turn the tide. If we won, there would be talk that the domination was over; if they won, it would continue. They had dominated us long enough, but it wouldn't be enough merely to prove we could compete with them on a more equal basis. We wanted four wins. Anything less would be a disappointment. Our job would not be complete.

I looked forward to the excitement of doing something team-oriented rather than self-oriented. I know my pitching in the stretch helped the team win, but that was a personal record. The camaraderie I felt with the Dodger players and coaches made me want to see us win, all of us. You can set records on your own (with a lot of help), but you win championships and Series only as a team.

The prospect of facing Dwight Gooden was exciting too, not that it makes any difference to my pitching performance. Except for the fact that he usually keeps the score low, my strategy remains the same: think about the next pitch and nothing else. But with ace against ace in the opening game of a series, there's always more tension in the air. I had to downplay the idea of facing Gooden, because there were eight other men in their lineup who could really hit the ball. Gooden's no automatic out, either. Like me, he loves to hit, and unlike me, he's one of the best-hitting pitchers in baseball.

I'm a Gooden fan. (In fact, we traded autographed jerseys during the season.) He's smart, he's overpowering, and he has wonderful mechanics. He would come into town with a career 4–0 record (in six starts) at Dodger stadium, and an ERA of 0.32 against us. He was 3–0 in 1988. Facing him would just make it all that much more fun. I threw on three days' rest twice during the streak, so I was willing to do that again. I would pitch every time they gave me the ball, starting or relieving. My job would be to keep the little guys off the bases so the big sticks like Keith Hernandez, Darryl Strawberry, Kevin McReynolds, and Gary Carter wouldn't drive in a bunch of runs.

In the 11 games we had played against them in 1988 they had outscored us 49–18, and only John Shelby hit as high as .300 against them. We were a typical Dodger offense, scratching out a few runs at a time and trying to hold the other team with pitching and defense. The Mets were a big-inning team, hitting 152 homers for the season to our 99. One thing was certain: this would be my toughest start of the season. The Mets led the league in runs scored, home runs, and RBIs. They had been shut out only four times all year.

It pumped me up to read and hear what the Mets were saying about the prospect of facing us. Strawberry said I had had a fine year but that the streak had come in September, "when some teams aren't playing their regular players. I don't mean to take anything away from him, but he'll be facing a more experienced lineup." Strawberry would come into the playoffs with 39 homers and 101 RBIs, leading a club that had six players in double figures for home runs. Kevin McReynolds had 98 RBIs.

Met catcher Gary Carter said it was likely that the law of averages would catch up with me. Howard Johnson, who was scheduled to start at shortstop, said the Mets were not intimidated by anyone. "We've faced hot guys before and beat them."

Second baseman Wally Backman said I hadn't thrown any of my streak innings against the Mets, so "we have a pretty good idea of how to beat him." Met manager Davey Johnson felt the opening game was crucial. He said the Mets feel better against a team they have had success with, "but if we don't win the first game, all that momentum we built during the season goes right out the window." Keith Hernandez agreed. "The first game is very important. If we can beat them and Hershiser, it will have to make them think. But if they win, it would help their confidence against us."

Our guys had a few things to say, too. Gibby said that by the numbers and the experts, "we might as well pack it in now. But if we had listened to the experts in the spring, we would have packed it in then. This team has shown we don't pay attention to all that. We seem to answer every bell that's rung."

Hatcher was hoping the Mets would think we had

little chance. "By our not getting any credit early this year, there was no pressure on us. If nobody expects us to win this thing, it might help. All year long we've believed we could win. It was something you could feel.

"Hey, if this team can win the division this year, anything is possible."

PART FIVE

THE POST-SEASON

16

DRAMA IN THE OPENER

The most sane comment we heard about our chances against the Mets came, for some reason, from Montreal manager Buck Rodgers, who didn't put as much stock as everyone else did in our 1–10 regular season record against New York. "They've both got great starting pitching—maybe a slight edge to the Mets there," he told the press. "The Mets have a little better offense, but the Dodgers have the better defense . . . I think it'll be a great series. [The regular season record] doesn't make any difference—unless the Dodgers think too much about it."

How could we do otherwise? It's all we heard about. We were glad the opener finally came. Waiting for such big games is like waiting for Christmas. You wait and wait and wonder if it'll ever come. Then finally it's upon you. My pre-game regimen took on a whole new aura with more than 55,000 fans rocking in the stands. The press swarmed the field during batting practice. After the typical intro-

151

duction of all the players from both teams, finally it was time for baseball. When I finished my warm-up tosses and stood behind the mound, my back to the leadoff hitter, there was no more talk, no more hype, no more expert opinion. There were no Mets, no Dodgers, no hitters. There was only the next pitch.

I took off my cap, and as is my custom before a game, I lifted a quick silent prayer of thanks for the opportunity and requests that no one get hurt and that we do our best. I had done everything I could think of to convince myself this was just a normal game. Excitement and adrenalin can't make you a better pitcher. The key is to focus, to concentrate, to keep doing what you do best—make the next pitch.

When I turned to look for the first sign, the Dodger crowd roared, and we were off.

With one out, rookie Gregg Jefferies—one of the youngest post-season players ever—singled on the first pitch. It was only the first of his three hits for the evening, proof that I had trouble figuring him out—and that he shows signs of being quite a hitter. The always-dangerous Keith Hernandez lined out hard to Tracy Woodson at first for a double play that got me out of the inning. I left the mound believing the tide had finally turned.

For once the breaks were going our way. I was uncomfortable on the mound. I wasn't hitting my spots, not feeling in the groove. I seemed to have good pop on the ball, but my confidence in individual pitches wasn't there yet. It caused me to be too careful, and with a lineup like that of the Mets, I was afraid that would catch up with me.

To get out of the top of the first inning with a single and then a line drive right at someone off the bat of one of the best hitters in baseball, well that pumps you up. I told the guys on the bench, "The tide has turned. Things have changed. It's going to go our way."

We jumped ahead early when Steve Sax led off with a single, stole second, and scored when Mike Marshall's broken bat single to right dropped in front of Strawberry.

My first at bat came in the third with no one on. Facing Dwight Gooden is like going to the dentist. You know you have to, but you'd rather be somewhere else. I ran the count to 3–2 and realized the chances of my getting a hit off Gooden were slim and none. The infield was playing back, so I flirted with laying down a bunt for a hit. Besides surprising the Mets, it would be impertinent enough to get our crowd and our team into the ball game. I squared around late but the ball sailed and I pulled back. Ball four. Gooden was mad.

I took a few steps off first, and Hernandez made no attempt to keep me close. They expected little from me in the way of base running. Gooden has always been easier than most pitchers, so on the first pitch I thought about going. When he threw a curve, I realized I could have made it. Frustrating! What a statement that would have been! But now Hernandez was onto me. He jogged to the bag, whistling and chirping comments like he always does.

"Hey, Doc, watch out. There's a crafty German over here making some moves." Always intense but usually friendly, he leaned toward me. "I thought you were only worried about pitching, big boy."

"Well, we gotta get *something* goin' here. One run isn't gonna do it against you guys."

"Not even with you on the mound?"

I laughed.

Gooden pitched his way out of that inning. We didn't get another hit until the seventh when Sosh got around on Gooden quicker than anyone had and lined a double down the right field line. He moved to third on a groundout, then scored on Alfredo Griffin's bloop single over the pulled-in infield.

Though he had scattered four hits and struck out ten, Gooden was lifted in the eighth for a pinch hitter. The last thing I was thinking about was that I had not been scored on since the fifth inning on August 30, but when we found ourselves leading the Mets 2–0 going into the ninth inning, we believed we would come out of the opener a quick game ahead.

Jefferies, my young nemesis, drove a solid single to lead off the inning. I felt good about getting Hernandez to ground out to first on a hit-and-run, though he did hit the ball as hard as Jefferies and moved the rookie into scoring position with one out.

Despite the fact that Jefferies came into the playoffs with a .321 average and future superstar written all over him, his lack of experience almost gave us an incredible break. He had not realized that Hernandez' grounder to first had been fair, and in his confusion after the play he wandered off second, back toward first. Griffin slipped in behind him and waved for the ball, hoping to catch him off base, but the throw never came. The screaming Mets got Jefferies' attention, and he moved back onto the bag. I can still taste that situation. We would have had two out and no one on, a much easier way to face Darryl Strawberry.

With first base open and only one out, I'm careful with Strawberry. Though he hasn't gotten the ball out of the infield in three previous at bats, he's the tying run, so I don't want to give him much to hit. If I walk him, that's better than letting him tie the game. If he hits the ball but it stays in the ballpark, we're still ahead. I couldn't know until later that right then the television network put a graphic on the screen indicating that I had never pitched a complete game win against the Mets.

Sosh comes out and we talk about his not moving too quickly into position to receive the pitch so we can keep Jefferies from signaling location to Strawberry. We also discuss changing the signals and what pitches I want to throw. In our dugout, Tommy is pacing. In the other dugout, the Mets have their hats on backward. Rally hats.

With the count 2–2, Strawberry fouls off two pitches. Then I hang a curveball. Stupid! Strawberry nearly jumps off the ground going after it. Lucky for me, he fouls this one off too. Still 2–2. Sosh throws the ball back to me and steps out in the front of the plate. I take the throw and turn my back to him. I'm not being mean, but I know the pitch was bad, wrong location, poor execution. I don't need to be reminded.

Okay, I hung it and threw a bad one. He fouled it off. If I throw the same exact pitch at the same trajectory, but it's my good one and it breaks down in the dirt, he's out. He was out in front of that one, and he'll be out in front of this one.

The adrenalin was pumping, and I should have known I would overthrow. I knew the moment I released the pitch that I was trying to break the ball too big. I gave it room to break, but in throwing the ball harder, it didn't have as much time to break, so it wound up in the same spot as the previous pitch. When I'm throwing that hard I need to aim for a shorter breaking ball, especially if I want to get it in the dirt.

I threw that ball with better spin and a better release point, but I threw it too hard. The first one had come in on the right trajectory but had the wrong spin and wasn't tight enough. The second one needed more snap, and I needed to get on top of it. Which I did, but with too much velocity.

Two hanging curves in a row. You don't get away with mistakes like that against a hitter like Strawberry. He drives the ball to center and winds up at second while Jefferies scores.

Suddenly, I'm history. On his way to the mound, Perranoski informs the umpire of the double switch. José Gonzalez will be a defensive replacement and bat in my spot. Before any dialogue on the mound, I know I'm out. The first run has been scored on me in more than 67 innings, I made three or four bad pitches in a row, and it's time to bring in our stopper, Jay Howell.

The press tried to make a big thing out of my getting pulled at that point. The fact is, it was the right move. I said and I meant that I had no problem with it. It made sense. I had thrown 99 pitches. I was not tired. I had not choked. But I *had* been hit hard three times and had made mistakes with the last two pitches. Baseball sense tells you it's time to shut the door with a hard-throwing reliever.

I was so mad at myself for those pitches to Strawberry that I hardly noticed the ovation as I trudged toward the dugout. It had been a long time since I had been lifted from a game. The run, as it related to all the scoreless innings I had pitched, didn't bother me. As it related to the game itself, it bothered me a lot. A shutout was irrelevant. I wanted to win this game for my team. We needed it. Allowing the Mets a breakthrough run in the ninth inning is bad business. Now we led just 2–1.

With first base open Jay pitched carefully to Kevin McReynolds, the heavy-hitting outfielder, and walked him. You hate to put the go-ahead run on, but you'd rather face Howard Johnson and Gary Carter than let McReynolds beat you with the homer.

Johnson strikes out. Two down. If we can get Carter, it's over. Carter goes to 0–2 on two curveballs. The place is jumping. Fans are on their feet. Have we turned the tide? Have we stopped the miracle Mets? Jay fires another curve, low and outside, and Carter goes after it with a desperate, lame-duck swing, breaks his bat, and lifts a dying fly ball to shallow center. Shelby was playing deep to protect against a double that would score both runs. With a late start, he's on the move, charging toward the ball. Strawberry and McReynolds, with two out, are circling the bases at top speed.

Shelby dives. No! It's off his glove. Strawberry scores. Shelby comes up with the ball, double pumps as McReynolds charges home, all 6–2 and 210 pounds of him. Sosh blocks the plate, McReynolds levels him. The throw is late. Unbelievably, maddeningly, miraculously again, the Mets lead 3–2. Down 2–1 with two outs and 0–2 on a .250 hitter, they manage to pull ahead. Is it possible we're jinxed? Can we beat them for 26 outs and never put them away?

We failed to score in the bottom of the ninth and suffered our bitterest defeat of the year.

The experts had great fun with that one. Many said I never should have been taken out, but look at the facts: That decision was right until Carter hit a good pitch, broke his bat, and blooped one to center. That decision took us to within one pitch of a 2–1 victory. Howell did what he was supposed to do. He didn't let McReynolds beat him, and he threw three mean pitches to Carter.

I tried to tell everybody that there was enough to criticize earlier in the game—times we didn't execute, didn't get the bunt down, didn't move the runner up—so we shouldn't lay the whole debacle at the feet of those who saw the lead slip away in the ninth.

I kicked myself mentally for hours over hanging those two curveballs. I know that sounds too hard on myself after the season I'd had and the game I'd pitched. But I get paid to make good pitches, not to make two mistakes in a row. I kept replaying in my mind that if I had not allowed the hit to Strawberry, we never would have been in that mess.

I stayed up for hours that night, wondering aloud to Jamie why I hung two curveballs in a row. What was my thought pattern? After the first I knew I needed to make a correction, then I got the same signal and came back and threw another one just like it. What happened? What adjustment had I not made?

"It's not your fault, Honey," Jamie would say.

"Yes, it is!"

"You can't take the blame for that loss."

"Maybe you're right. We came within one strike, and Tommy made the right move."

But then I'd think about it some more. "I wasn't tired, and I shouldn't have hung that pitch!"

There's more than second-guessing. You don't admit it to the press, but you do start wondering if it isn't the same old thing. We can't beat these guys. Something goes their way every time. All we wanted to do was start with a clean slate, begin positively, beat them, and show everyone it was a new day. We had done it until the last pitch.

The media also made a big deal of how that was the Dodgers' fifth straight post-season loss, because we had dropped four straight to the Cardinals in 1985—as if this was by any stretch the same Dodger team. But that didn't hurt as much as Met manager Davey Johnson's comment: "For Los Angeles to change the momentum, which they needed, they had to win game one. We felt if we could beat Hershiser, it would keep things going our way. Now there's more pressure for Los Angeles to win."

That made Tommy Lasorda mad. "Since when is this a one-game playoff?" he said. "Last I heard, you have to win four. They haven't done anything but win one!"

Later Tommy told me:

"When we lost that first game, we could have very easily been destroyed. There was nobody more dejected and depressed than me when I left that ballpark. That hurt me a great deal. I had to go out and eat dinner with my relatives, which I didn't want to do. I got up the next day and had to take some friends and relatives to lunch, which I didn't want to do. I was the most miserable guy in the world.

"The next night, when I walked into the clubhouse, Doug Krikorian [columnist for the *Herald-Examiner*] was sitting in my office. I walked in hollering, 'We're gonna get these guys! We're gonna get 'em, beat 'em! What do ya say, boys?'

"Krikorian says to me, 'I can't believe you. After that loss last night, your enthusiasm today?'

"I said, 'Let me tell you something: There's no one any more dejected and depressed than I am. But when I walk through that clubhouse door, I gotta put on a new face. I gotta put on a winning face. I gotta put on a happy face, because if my players see me depressed, that's going to be the attitude and the atmosphere around here.'

"At the team meeting, I said, 'If this is a one-game playoff, we're out. Huh? Is it a one-game playoff? Are we out? We win tonight, we bounce back from a very tough loss.'"

What we were about to find out was that the Mets' brash young starter for that game, the brilliant, flame-throwing David Cone (who had gone 20–3 for the year), had already given us all the incentive we needed to beat him.

17

HANGING TOUGH

I don't think rookie starter Tim Belcher needed any more incentive than the maddening way we had lost the night before, but if he had, it was provided by David Cone of the Mets. The 21-year-old, second-year man had written in his New York newspaper column exactly what he and the Mets thought of us, and it had been posted in our clubhouse.

Some samples:

"Ever heard the saying 'Better to be lucky than good?' Trash it, because Hershiser was just lucky. Look what happened to luck in the ninth inning last night. It's called justice—catching up to luck and pummeling it into the ground. Trouble was, Orel was lucky for eight innings.

"I'll tell you a secret: As soon as we got Orel out of the game, we knew we'd beat the Dodgers. Knew it even after Jay Howell had struck out HoJo [Howard Johnson]. We saw Howell throwing curveball after curveball and we were thinking, *this* is the Dodgers' idea of a stopper? Our idea is Randy [Myers], a guy who can blow you away with his heat. Seeing Howell and his curveball reminded us of a high school pitcher.

"This is a heartbreaker for the Dodgers. I won't say this breaks their spirit. Not yet. But this hurts them. So, tonight, my moment comes. I've waited for it. I've freeze-framed the image a thousand times. Cone stands on the mound. Cone takes a deep breath. Cone winds up. Cone throws a . . . what?"

Here's what. In the first two innings, we scored five runs on five hits (four of which Cone would later say were "seeing-eye hits. I don't think that newspaper article made those grounders find holes").

Meanwhile, Timmy Belcher, 6 feet 3 inches tall and 210 pounds with a good fastball and a sharp slider, was pitching a great game, especially for a rookie under such pressure. He allowed just five hits and struck out a season-high 10, going into the ninth inning with a 6–2 lead. He gave up a double to Lenny Dykstra and, after an out, faced Keith Hernandez, who had hit a two-run homer for the Mets in the fourth. Hernandez drove in Dykstra with a single, making it 6–3, and left-hander Jesse Orosco (a former Met) came in to face Strawberry.

Belcher was upset about being taken out and thrashed around in the dugout before I got a chance to talk with him. "Don't worry about the ninth, Timmy," I said. "You did your job. You gave us a chance to win. You did what you were supposed to do."

Orosco gave up a single to Strawberry, and suddenly we all had visions of the night before. But Alejandro Peña came in to get the final two outs, and the series was even, heading to New York for the next three games.

To David Cone's credit, the next day he admitted that his comments in the paper had come after an emotional victory, that he was not going to hide or blame the words on a ghost-writer. "I meant my words to be facetious and I should've communicated that better. It was poor judgment. If I had to write my column again, I would have said Jay Howell is an all-star who throws a great curve. I didn't mean any disrespect to Jay. . . ."

All it had done, as some of our guys said, was toss gas on our fire. And we were fired up. Of course, revenge is no motivator. It doesn't make you throw or hit any better. But we were sure glad to be going to New York dead even instead of down by two. There are few things harder than beating the Mets two of three at their own ballpark.

A fragile John Tudor was scheduled to pitch game three, but it was rained out. The Belcher victory, the travel day, and the rainout gave me three days' rest, and all of a sudden I was the new starter for the first game in New York.

Tommy Lasorda was asked if the rain delay had been an advantage for the Dodgers, now that he could use me for a second start in three games. He wasn't so sure. "I don't know where the advantage lies, I really don't," he said. "When you start thinking a rained-out game gives you an advantage, it can backfire on you. We're very happy we can use Orel today and that we can give Tudor a little while longer to get stronger."

Three days' rest for me is more of a blessing that a detriment, because when I feel good, when I'm in a groove, I'd rather have the ball than sit around. Despite the fact that I had not earned a decision in game one, I had pitched eight innings of shutout ball and had made only a few bad pitches in the ninth. I still felt sharp. I was ready.

The problem was, the third game never should have been played. Not that day, anyway. It was so cold and rainy in New York, and the field was in such poor shape that I'm convinced the only reason the game was played was because it was a playoff and we had to fit it into the schedule. Two consecutive rainouts after a travel day would have botched up everything. Meanwhile, Oakland was making short work of the Red Sox, so the A's were likely going to win the American League championship and have plenty of rest before the World Series. We had to play on.

Shea Stadium was so muddy and sloppy it was like playing in a pig sty. The tarp had protected the field before we started, but by the fourth inning it was like a soup bowl. With the temperature in the forties, I wore long underwear, my longsleeved sweatshirt, and a dickey.

A lot of our guys moaned about having to play at all, but it was the same for both teams. I tried to encourage them, saying that whoever was the toughest was going to win.

Early on I had trouble with my footing. You tend to be careful trying to plant your front foot on a muddy mound, and it affected my motion. I also had trouble finding a solid grip on the ball. Perry came out and told me to concentrate on pitching, not on all the mechanical things affected by the weather. He reminded me that I wasn't bending my back enough because my footing was tentative. I knew that would give me more control, but I didn't want to slip, either.

Hitters tried to keep the barrel of the bat dry by wiping it between their legs or under their arms. After every half inning the grounds crew spread on the infield something called Diamond Dry, which is a sort of dust-mixture that soaks up the moisture and is supposed to improve footing.

Ahead 3–1, I faced Keith Hernandez leading off the bottom of the sixth. One of the things that makes him such a tough hitter (he has a lifetime batting average of over .300) is that he has somehow developed the knack of fouling off pitches when he needs to. I don't know if it's something he practices or what, but when he's behind in the count and looking for a pitch to drive, if he gets fooled or if a pitch looks like a strike but isn't the one he wants, he'll foul it off more often than not.

He wound up singling into center field, but when he tried to advance to third on a hit by Strawberry, he slipped in the muck and crawled into the tag. One out, man on first. McReynolds hit a grounder to third, but the throw from Jeff Hamilton to Mickey Hatcher at first was in the dirt. Hatcher came up with it, but first base umpire Dutch Rennert ruled that he trapped the ball against his chest and didn't have control of it. Tommy and Mickey argued long and hard, but the replay clearly shows the call was right.

With men on first and second and one out, we retired Howard Johnson. Now Gary Carter was the hitter. He had beat us in game one and was the last hitter Peña had faced in game two. I needed this out.

It was cold and miserable, but I was in the game. I convinced myself that this was just like spring training with nobody on. The only thing that matters is execution, the next pitch. If I allowed myself to dwell on the do-or-die importance of every pitch, I'd be good for nothing on the mound. Who could perform with that pressure?

Carter slapped a single into right, scoring Strawberry and moving McReynolds to third, so now it's 3–2 with two down and Backman coming up. He grounds one between first and second, and I'm running over to cover first, I see Hatcher get a glove on the ball, slowing it before it gets to Sax. Safe all around, game tied, 3–3.

That's the way it stood going into the bottom of the seventh. There was no use brooding over what had happened in the sixth because I had not been hit hard. I also felt lucky about the Hernandez out after he had slipped in the mud. On a dry day, he might have even scored.

Mookie Wilson led off the seventh drawing a walk on a good pitch I thought could have been called either way. Then I had to face Jefferies, who'd been hitting me like he owned me. He was five for nine in the series at that point, so I had to bear down. I was glad to see him square around to bunt and try to move the great base-running Wilson to second, because I didn't know what to throw him if he was hitting away. I was thinking, *I'm sure glad you're bunting, because I can't get you out.*

Eventually he moved Wilson to second on a hit-and-run, and here came Hernandez. This lineup never quits coming at you. We intentionally walked Hernandez to set up the force, and Perranoski came out to see how I was doing and whether I wanted to stay in and pitch to Strawberry. "We've got Orosco warming up."

"I can get him, Perry," I said.

At this stage in my career and with the success I had at the end of the season, that's all Perry needed to hear. I immediately set about proving myself wrong by running the count to 3–0 on Strawberry, the most dangerous hitter in the league (he was hitting .455 in the playoffs at the time).

First and second, one out, 3–3 in the game, series tied at one. I can't give in to Strawberry, but he's not swinging. I say to myself, "Well, Darryl, it's you and me. Here we go. It's comin' down the middle. You're either gonna get a hit or make an out. We're about to find out."

Checked swing. Ump says he went around. 3–1. Same scenario. Same pitch. Strength against strength. I have no place to put him. I can't walk him and put the go-ahead run on third. If I throw a ball, he has a 100 percent chance of getting on base. If I throw a strike, he has a one-in-three chance of getting a hit. Even if the best hitter in history was up there, the odds are 2–1 in the pitcher's favor. Those percentages should make a pitcher more confident and aggressive. Here it comes. Ground ball! Double play! We're out of the inning.

In the top of the eighth we loaded the bases and Tommy had Danny Heep pinch hit for me. We had to go for the runs. They countered with Randy Myers on the mound, so Tommy switched and hit Mike Sharperson. He walked to drive in the go-ahead run. Now I could be the winning pitcher, but

I couldn't lose it. That's a good situation for me, but it's meaningless if we don't hang on.

Tim Leary caught me in the locker room after I got taken out. "What were you thinking when you had Strawberry 3–1 and you knew you couldn't walk him?"

"I was just thinking, *Here it comes.*"

"That's what I thought you were thinking. That's what I would have been thinking."

Jay Howell came in to relieve in the bottom of the eighth and faced Kevin McReynolds who was 0 for 3 in the game and 0 for 10 in the series. Overdue.

Ball one.

Ball two.

Ball three.

Foul. Strike one.

Foul. Strike two.

But then here came Davey Johnson. Joe West, the plate umpire, approached the mound and asked to see Jay's glove. Demper and Tommy and another umpire, Harry Wendelstedt, joined them. There was pine tar (normally used for a better grip on the bat) on Jay's glove. Will McReynolds be awarded first base? Will Jay be asked to wash pine tar off his hand?

No! He was ejected. It was unbelievable.

I thought Davey Johnson had Howell checked because he saw him going to his glove between pitches. Maybe Davey was hoping to get a ball called or in some way throw Jay off. I think it surprised even the Mets when Jay was ejected.

There is no way that Jay was trying to affect the rotation or flight of the ball by using pine tar. It was a miserable, wet night and there's no question in my mind that he was using it for a better grip. The umps know that, and I thought they would maybe call the last pitch a ball and make Jay either get rid of the excess pine tar on his glove or his fingers.

After Jay was ejected the umpires took the glove to the box of National League president Bart Giamatti, who was sitting with Ed Vargo, supervisor of umpires. It got to be a real show. We felt bad for Jay, but we had a game to win. Alejandro Peña came on in relief.

Wally Backman tied the game with a double, driving in Howard Johnson, who had reached first on a fielder's choice. Backman scored the go-ahead run after pinch hitter Lenny Dykstra walked and Mookie Wilson singled off Jesse Orosco. Jefferies was hit by a pitch, and with the bases loaded Hernandcz walked to pushed another run across. The Mets scored twice more in the inning, giving them five in the eighth and a 8–4 lead, which is how it ended.

I had pitched 15 innings in the series without a decision.

We were down two games to one with two more to play in New York, but the worst news came when Jay Howell was suspended for three games. We agreed with Tommy Lasorda that the whole incident was uncalled for. If there was too much pine tar, sure, something had to be done. But no way was Jay Howell trying to cheat. We know him better than that.

Tommy says, "Pine tar does absolutely nothing to the flight of the ball. It's used strictly to get a better grip, the same as the rosin bag. A chemist told me that pine tar is nothing but a liquid from of rosin. I spoke my mind about the ruling, not because I have any problem with what the league office decides, but because I want the world to know that my pitcher is not a cheater. If he had scuffed the ball, if he had sandpapered the ball, if he had done anything to that baseball, that to me would have been deserving of being kicked out and suspended, but not this.

"Not once during the entire year that Jay Howell pitched for the Dodgers did a hitter step out and question the flight of the ball."

What were we going to do for a stopper for the rest of the series?

18

"I'LL BE YOUR JAY HOWELL"

Before facing Dwight Gooden in game four the next day, it was time for another of Tommy's pep talks. He told us we were a team with character, a team that had had its back up against the wall before. "Every time we've been in this situation, you've come through, and you're gonna do it again today. Losing Jay [Howell] is a tough blow to this ballclub, but we can *not* let it stop us. We're gonna win this ball game, with or without Jay Howell."

As the players filed out, I told Tommy, "Hey, Skip, I'll be your Jay Howell tonight." He gave me a look like he wanted to hug me, but I also read something else in his eyes. True, with Howell out and tomorrow's starter Tim Belcher resting at the hotel, Tommy had only seven pitchers available. But he also knew I had thrown 110 pitches in seven innings the day before. He didn't say anything. He just slapped me on the back. Reporters asked him if he would use me if he got low on pitchers.

"No, no, no way," he said.

Our starter John Tudor, Kirk Gibson, and a few others had written JH on their sleeves. We wanted Jay to know we were with him and that he hadn't let the team down.

In the top of the first, Sax led off with an infield hit and then stole second. Hatcher walked. Both scored when Shelby drove a broken-bat single into right field. We hoped Gooden wouldn't find his normal groove.

Tudor took that 2–0 lead into the bottom of the fourth when Keith Hernandez led off with a bloop single. Darryl Strawberry tied the game on the next pitch with a shot to the bullpen that was gone the instant it left his bat. Two pitches later Kevin McReynolds duplicated the feat from the right side, and we trailed 3–2.

We knew McReynolds would be trouble. He had finished the season with a September that saw him hit .345 with seven homers and 22 RBIs. He led off the sixth with a double and scored on Gary Carter's follow-up triple. That was all for Tudor, whose hip was bothering him. Brian Holton came on and held Carter at third on a strikeout, a walk, and a double play. It was a great bit of pitching often overlooked when people reminisce about that game.

Our hopes of catching Gooden on an off night were short-lived. He was dominant, having struck out 10 and not given up a hit since the first when we came to bat in the top of the ninth. Our bench was dejected. We were down 4–2, in danger of falling behind 3–1 in games with one left in New York and—we hoped—two in Los Angeles. We were always optimistic, but there was no one on that bench who didn't know what we were up against.

John Shelby led off the ninth taking two high pitches for a rare walk after running the count to 2–2. Sosh was up next. He'd gone 2 for 14 off Gooden during the season and had hit .167 against the Mets. But he *had* gotten around good on him for a double to right earlier in the series. Now he was guessing Gooden would try to get ahead on the count after giving up a walk. He guessed right. The contact hitter, who had only three home runs all year and one since June 27, lined the first pitched just over the right field wall. Suddenly we were alive, tied 4–4.

We were getting fantastic relief pitching from our bullpen, including Ricky Horton and Alejandro Peña (who would throw three hitless innings). In the bottom of the tenth, Sosh was the hero again, ending the inning by throwing out Mookie Wilson on a steal attempt with Strawberry at the plate. Imagine what could have happened if Wilson had been safe or if the throw had gone into center and he had wound up on third.

In the bottom of the eleventh, the Mets threatened again when McReynolds and Bachman walked. With two down Peña got Johnson to popout. It was going to be a long night. When Tim Leary got up in the bullpen and started warming up for the twelfth, I went to Perry. "I'm ready to pitch if you need me."

"Are you kidding? After seven innings in the cold yesterday?"

"Timmy's our last right hander. Today's the day to use me. You know I don't get stiff until the second day after a start. I'm not making the decision for you, but I'm going down there. I'll be ready." Perry didn't answer. He didn't even look at me. I felt like an obnoxious kid trying to wear down a parent.

I always want to relieve, and I bug Tommy and Perry to death about it. They get tired of hearing from me, and they tell me I can't do everything, that it would insult the bullpen to imply the relievers can't handle the job, and that I should just rest or workout on my off days. But I never give up asking and volunteering. "I'm fine," I say. "My arm feels good. I can relieve tonight if you need me. The bullpen is tired."

Usually Perry or Tommy tells me, "It's not a good risk. We don't want to mess up the rotations." But I love to play. I love to be out there. *I love to pitch.*

I jogged down the tunnel, into the clubhouse and straight to my locker. In the corner, several guys who had already been in the game were watching us on television, hitting in the top of the twelfth. I got my cup on and changed into my spikes.

"What do you think you're doing?" someone said.

"Gettin' ready to pitch. If Gibson hits one out, they might need me."

Gibby was at the plate against Roger McDowell with no one on. McDowell had given up a game-winning homer only once in 1988. Gibson had had a tough night, striking out twice and grounding out three times. He was only one for 16 in the series so far. Back in May he had hit an extra inning homer in the fourteenth against the Cubs. During that same week I had worked my only inning in relief— pitching the twelfth for a save against the Cubs.

The guys erupted when Gibby crushed a fastball and drove it all the way to the scoreboard, about 430 feet from the plate. We led 4–3. "Nice prediction," someone shouted. I didn't react. I didn't even watch the replay. I could feel my game face coming on, and I headed directly to the bullpen.

When I got there, Beach [bullpen coach, Mark Cresse] said, "What are you doing here?"

"I'm here to get ready."

"What?!"

He got on the phone to Perry in the dugout. "Bulldog's down here. What do you want me to do with him? Let him be? Okay."

Beach shrugged.

"Let me try my arm," I said. "Tell me what you think, you know, after yesterday. I want to be able to give them a legitimate answer if they ask me."

"I gotta get permission."

He's back on the phone, and this time Tommy answers. "Bulldog wants to throw. Should I let him?"

Beach hangs up and grabs his glove. "Come on. He said you can throw easy."

I didn't think about the fact that the television cameras would pick that up, and the announcers would get excited about last night's starter throwing in the bullpen. As I began to loosen up, I felt good. Meanwhile Tim Leary was getting into trouble on the mound. Mackey Sasser and Lee Mazzilli both singled, but after Gregg Jefferies flied out to left, here came the heart of the Mets order: Hernandez, Strawberry, and McReynolds. Every Dodger, me included, thought back to that first game and the excruciating three-run ninth that resurrected New York from a 2–0 death.

Here's what happened next, from Tommy's perspective:

"Leary doesn't look like he's got good stuff, and I'm thinkin' we're gonna blow this game after we played so hard and had such great relief pitchin', especially from Horton and Peña, and then Scoscia got that big home run. Worse than that, we're gonna be down 3–1 in games.

"Even though Orosco had a bad outing the night before, I look over at Perranoski and I say, 'If I'm gonna manage this club right, I gotta bring in the left-hander to pitch to these two lefties. Go get Leary and bring in Orosco.'

"Perry says to me, 'Wait a minute. We don't have anybody left after that. You bring in Orosco, and we don't have any more pitchers.'

"I say, 'Go get him.'

"Hernandez is the hitter, first and second, one out, we got a one-run lead, bottom of the twelfth; it's now about ten to one in the morning. Orosco walks Hernandez on four pitches. He doesn't come close to throwin' a strike. Bases loaded.

"The first pitch to Strawberry is right in his wheelhouse. He jumps off both feet and takes such a tremendous cut that if he does more than just skin the ball, it goes to Long Island. Then three straight balls. I run out to the mound and tell Orosco, in effect, that if he knows how to throw a strike, now's the time to do it.

"He throws a strike, so now it's three and two. And I say to Perranoski, 'Ronnie, do you think the Lord will make it possible for this guy to strike out or pop up? Because if He does, I'm bringin' in the Bulldog.'

"Perranoski says nothing, and Strawberry pops up to Saxy. I say to Ron, 'Go get 'im.'

" 'Tommy! The guy pitched seven innings last night! What if they tie the game? How long can he go? He's all we've got!'

" 'They're not gonna tie this game. I'm puttin' the pot of gold on the Bulldog. Go get 'im!' "

From the bullpen I can see Perry leave the dugout. I throw a few more pitches at full tilt, and then Cresse says, "You're in there."

I'm in? It was what I volunteered for. I had told them all year that if they ever needed me in relief, I could do it. And now they needed me. For the briefest instant I couldn't believe what was about to happen, what I had gotten myself into. I had badgered my way into the most dramatic, most difficult situation possible. The last several minutes raced past my mind's eye: saying I would be ready, changing into my game uniform, predicting Gibby's home run, being the last pitcher on the staff, warming up, Perranoski coming out of the dugout, Cresse saying, "You're in," and now I'm pawing the dirt in the bullpen. What have I gotten myself into?

We need this game like no other we've ever needed. It's Shea Stadium; not one of the more than 50,000 fans has left. It's the bottom of the twelfth, the bases are loaded, two are out, and we're up by one. With zero days' rest I'm going to face Kevin McReynolds, one of the most powerful hitters in the National League.

I told myself, "You can't be thinking like this. You have one job and only one job, and that's the next pitch." McReynolds has hit a homer and a double already; it's time to think about pitch selection. Just like that, the distractions were gone. I forgot the crowd, I forgot my predicament, I forgot any twinge of fear or foreboding. I would not think of failing. I would execute.

"All right, you've got yourself into it, now you've got to do it." We all know people who go through life avoiding challenges, and others who take challenges but back off when the going gets tough. Then there are those who find the courage to rise to the occasion. It's not that they're unafraid. But to me, courage means carrying on in spite of fear and never retreating. I was afraid, but I was not looking back.

As I emerged from the bullpen, there were oohs and aahs from the crowd, then a chorus of boos. Someone held up a banner that read: *Orel Who*? I was pumped up. I was thinking about pitching. There was no room to put McReynolds. There would be no fooling around out there. I couldn't risk bouncing a curveball, because a wild pitch would mean a run. It would be sandlot ball, strength against strength.

I looked into the Mets' dugout. I knew what I'd be thinking if they brought *their* ace in to relieve with no days' rest. I'd know they really wanted this game. I rearranged the dirt in front of the mound and paced on the grass, getting myself acclimated to the situation and reminding myself of all the dangers and possibilities. I allowed myself to get worked up and to become that aggressive Orel Hershiser I need to be to get people out. I couldn't be the laid back, easygoing Orel now.

Tommy said later: "You talk about a guy prayin' in the dugout! All I can think of is that if the Bulldog walks a run in, allows a single, throws a wild pitch, hits a batter, anything that ties the game, I got nobody else who can pitch. For Bulldog's arm and my pitching staff, if he's gonna put someone on, it's almost better that he allows a hit that wins the game for the Mets. The only eligible pitcher I've got left is Belcher, and he's back at the hotel, ready to pitch the next day.

"I said, 'Lord, I'll tell Ya somethin'. Let Bulldog get this guy out, and I'll never ask Ya for anything again.'"

As I took my warm-up pitches, I threw as hard as I had all year. I was psyched. I knew I had no more than six or seven pitches to throw, even if McReynolds fouled off a few. There was nothing to save myself for. It was do or die, Russian Roulette. If they tied the game I would have to pitch all night, or until we could get Timmy Belcher to the stadium from the hotel. But that wasn't going to happen. No, the game was right here in front of me with a bat in his hand.

My arm felt great, the adrenalin was pumping. There was no pain. My mechanics were excellent. Everything was flowing. The umpire waved McReynolds into the box and I stared in for the sign. Demper called for a hard sinker away. I threw it as hard as I could. McReynolds looked it over. It wasn't as "away" as it was supposed to be. Strike one.

The next pitch was a ball. I flirted with coming back with a curve, but I didn't want to go to 2–1 and let him know there was a fastball coming. I had the advantage that he might be expecting a curve, so I decided to go with the fastball with as much movement as I could put on it.

The call was for another fastball away, but I already knew what I was going to throw. I tried to get on top of it and get my arm and my fingers in a position to throw it with the best speed and release point so it would ride in and sink. I wasn't worried about exact location; I figured if I threw the ball down the middle with movement, it wouldn't wind up there. I was right. The ball rode in on him. He swung and connected.

Tommy picks up the story again:

"McReynolds hits a ball that looks exactly like the one Carter hit to win game one in the same situation—a dying quail to center. Did you ever ride a human being the way a jockey rides a horse? I was ridin' John Shelby! I mean, it was like I was on his back with a whip, yellin', 'Come on! Come on!' Three base runners are movin' as fast as they can go, and Shelby catches that ball about this high off the ground [knee level]. We win 4–3."

I walked off the mound and thrust out my fist. "Yeah!" It was as demonstrative as I had ever been on the mound, but to that point that had been the most emotional moment of my career. Never before had so many elements contributed to a dramatic situation. Everything had ridden on one at-bat of an MVP-level hitter.

Tommy continues: "You talk about bedlam. You talk about players jumpin' up and down, players huggin' each other. Talk about winning an important game! How important was that game? It's now 2–2 in the playoffs instead of us down 3–1 with another game at Shea the next day. We were staring defeat right in the eyes. I mean, Orosco, had 3–1 on Strawberry with one out and two on.

"After the game, Perranoski comes to me in my office. 'I gotta ask you a question, Tommy,' he says. 'They tie that game, what do you do?'

"I looked him right in the eye. 'You promise you won't tell nobody?'

"'Yeah.'

"'My four brothers were in the ballpark. I'd have had 'em blow out the lights. There would have been no more baseball tonight.'

"Seriously, though, if the Mets tie that game, the Bulldog has to stay in till it's over, no matter what. And then what do people say about me doin' that to him—makin' a guy pitch another four or five innings after seven innings the night before? And if he gives up the winning hit, I look just as bad. Talk about puttin' your neck on the line. The Bulldog saved my hide."

Kirk Gibson said later that my performance in that game proved that I put the team ahead of myself. My motivation had been wanting to win. Ironically, I had pitched in three of the four National League Championship Series games and had two no-decisions and a save to show for it.

Now I just hoped we could win the next one in New York and the first one in Los Angeles after that. If we didn't, if we won only one, I was scheduled to start game seven in Los Angeles.

19

BRING ON THE A'S

Timmy Belcher retired the first ten Mets he faced in game five, while we took the lead in the top of the fourth off Sid Fernandez. Mike Marshall singled to center with one out. After John Shelby walked, they both scored on the first of Rick Dempsey's two doubles. Demper scored one out later when Alfredo Griffin doubled.

That 3–0 lead looked pretty good, the way Timmy was going. In the top of the fifth, however, we doubled it when Steve Sax and Mickey Hatcher singled and Kirk Gibson hit his second home run in two days. His 350–foot shot to right knocked Fernandez out of the box.

Down 6–0, the Mets came right back in the bottom of the fifth when Lenny Dykstra matched Gibson's three-run homer to right. Dykstra would also double in the eighth and score another run, but Mike Marshall's ninth inning RBI triple gave us a 7–4 lead, and that's how it ended.

The momentum had turned our way. Heading

back to Los Angeles, we needed just one more victory in the final two games to win the National League championship. Of course, we couldn't do it the easy way. David Cone and Kevin McReynolds had something to say about that.

Though he walked both Sax and Hatcher to lead off the game, Cone pitched a complete game, five-hit (all singles), one-run victory while McReynolds went four-for-four, including another double and homer and three RBIs. The Mets won 5–1.

The National League Championship Series was tied 3–3. We were glad the deciding game would be at Dodger Stadium. There was a sense of foreboding, however, because the troublesome Mets had a way of snatching victory from defeat. We'd had them down 2–0 in the ninth in the first game, and we lost. We'd led them three games to two coming back to Los Angeles, and we lost.

The start would be my fourth appearance in seven games. I would be going up against Ron Darling again, just like in game three. He had started and pitched the first six innings of that game, earning no decision, though the Mets won. Some tried to forecast that Gooden would start this game, and strangely enough, he wound up pitching more that night than any other Met.

I was in trouble in the top of the first when, with one out, Backman singled and Hernandez walked. Fortunately, I was able to get Strawberry on a second to short fielder's choice, and McReynolds ended the inning with a liner to Jeff Hamilton at third.

As he'd done so many times during the season, Sax got us started by getting on base and scoring. He singled to center and moved to third on Hatcher's double to left. Gibby drove Saxy in on a sacrifice fly to center. I had to hand it to Darling. He could have fallen apart right then with Hatcher on third and only one out, with Marshall and Shelby coming up. We thought we had Darling on the ropes, but he fanned them both.

I didn't expect a one-run lead to hold up, but I'll take what I can get. Like most pitchers, I'm a different man on the mound when I'm ahead. It's the old story of feeling free to take certain risks you wouldn't take otherwise. My only scare in the second came on a two-out single to right by Kevin Elster. The Mets were going to pester me with one hit in each of the first four innings. Fortunately, we were uncharacteristically explosive in the bottom of the second.

Sosh led off with a single to right. Jeff Hamilton (Hammy) followed with a single to left. Alfredo tried to move them both over with a sacrifice bunt, but he beat it out for a single and we had the bases loaded and nobody out. Guess who came to the plate in that crucial situation?

I pulled a one-hopper to Jefferies at third, but he couldn't get a handle on it. Sosh scored and the bases were still loaded. Saxy followed with his second of three singles to center for the night, driving in Hamilton and Griffin. I was held at second. With two on and nobody out, we led 4–0 and the Mets had to do something. Darling was lifted for Gooden. Now I really knew how the Mets felt when I was brought in in the bottom of the twelfth in game four. They were pulling out all the stops, and he was the best they had.

Hatcher grounded out second to first, pushing Sax

and me to second and third. When I got there, third baseman Jefferies needled me about causing his error. "How could you do that to me?"

"What happened?" I said. I had simply hit the ball and run.

"I just rushed the play," he said.

"Hang in there. That's baseball." I should have told him he deserved it after the way he had been hitting me. He would go two for four off me in that game to make it 6 for 11 in the series!

With first base open, Gibby was walked intentionally. Marshall followed with a groundball to second, but Backman erred on the throw. I scored our fourth run of the inning and fifth overall, Sax moved to third, Gibby to second, and of course Marshall was at first.

Shelby knocked in one more run with a sacrifice fly to left, also moving Gibson and Marshall up a base and leaving first open. Gooden intentionally walked Sosh, who had doubled and homered off him earlier in the series, and finally ended the onslaught by getting Hamilton on a called third strike. We had scored five in the inning, four earned, and led 6–0. We took the field to a standing ovation, but Tommy caught me as I left the dugout. "Don't let up! Go hard! Don't save anything! We've got somebody behind you if you can't make it!"

He needn't have worried. In my mind this was still a 1–0 game. Every pitch counted. I would go as hard as I could for as long as I could. Everything rested on executing the next pitch.

Gooden would retire six in a row over the next two innings, and we wouldn't score the rest of the way—despite threatening with two base runners in the sixth. But if I couldn't hold a six-run lead, I didn't belong on the mound.

A leadoff single to center by Dykstra in the third was erased with a double play, and in the next three innings I allowed only one base runner, Jefferies (of course), on a two-out single in the fourth. My second and third outs in the sixth were strikeouts of Strawberry and McReynolds. The key to beating the Mets is trying to contain those heavy hitters. In that game, though Dykstra, Backman, Jefferies, and Elster were five for 13 off me, Hernandez, Strawberry, and McReynolds were 0 for 11. Something tells me I haven't heard the last from those guys.

The Mets threatened in the seventh when Jefferies hit a one-out double to right and I wild-pitched him to third. I got out of the inning on two flyball outs, and suddenly we could taste it. We were going to win. We were going to beat the Mets. We were going to be National League champs and go to the World Series. After all the doom-saying and the hype about the incredible mismatch, the Dodgers were going to be more than just the best in the West.

With one out in the top of the eighth, I hit Dykstra with a pitch and walked Backman, but the last thing I wanted to do was to come out. I wanted to finish this one, to shut out the Mets. This one was for the team; it had nothing to do with a streak. This was the best team in the National League, but if we could hold on, they would be watching us in the World Series.

Oakland had made short work of Boston in the American League, drubbing them in four straight. Don Baylor of the A's had already been quoted that he hoped the Mets would win so the A's would be able to prove themselves against the best the National League had to offer. Can you imagine how motivating that was to us?

I settled down and got Hernandez and Strawberry on groundouts. Our last seven hitters had been retired in order by Met relievers, and I took the 6–0 lead into the top of the ninth. Dodger Stadium was rockin', nearly 56,000 people standing and cheering and waving. You can't fathom the energy from a crowd like that unless you're there to experience it. I had to stay in the game, keep my game face on, my mind on the next pitch.

McReynolds flied out to left. I finally got the pesky Jefferies on a groundball to short. Lee Mazzilli came in to pinch hit for the pitcher, and I quickly had him down 0–2. Here we were. Two out, ninth inning, up 6–0. I had scattered five hits, only one double, had struck out five and walked two.

I wanted to enjoy this. I took my time, let my game face slacken. *This is a moment I want to remember.* I looked around. The fans were on their feet, delirious with anticipation. The Dodgers in the dugout were on their feet, waving towels. smiling, shouting encouragement.

I took the rosin bag and tossed it down, letting the ovation build, stalling, staring long and hard at Sosh. Mazzilli was by no means an automatic out. He was one of the best pinch hitters in the National League and always seemed to come up with the clutch hit for the Mets. A hit wouldn't hurt us now, but I would have hated to let him break up the shutout with a dinger. Especially now that I had two strikes on him.

As I rubbed up the ball, I wasn't thinking of the

next pitch and only the next pitch. I was thinking how grateful I was to be there, to be healthy, to have had the year I had, to have enjoyed the guys on the team. God had blessed me by allowing this moment, the kind of experience any athlete at any level dreams about for years. I let it all inside, invading my zone, destroying my game face. I fought a smile and held back tears. This was going to be special, really special. One more pitch. Just one more.

Sosh called for a fastball in, and I know he wanted the one that sinks and moves away from the left-hand hitter, back toward the plate. I threw a four-seamer, the one that sails in toward the hitter and crowds him. I was so pumped and got so much on it that the ball cut too sharply and hit Mazzilli. As soon as I let it go I shouted, "Look out!" Mazzilli glared at me as he started toward first, but he softened when I said, "Hey, I'm sorry!" He had to know there was no reason for me to hit him on purpose with an 0–2 pitch in the bottom of the ninth of the championship game. He might have thought I was just doing it to be a jerk, to rub it in to the irritating Mets. But I wouldn't have done that, and when I apologized, he knew it. The best revenge is success, not retaliation.

Sosh jogged out to the mound. "What was that?"

"The fastball in."

"It was supposed to be a sinker!"

"I know, but I threw the cutter instead."

"I didn't want that! You might hit him!"

"I *did*!"

"Let's go!" he said. "Get back in the game!"

"Okay," I said. "Here's what we're gonna do. Tracy [Woodson] will play behind Mazzilli like he's not

gonna hold him on. I'll go into my windup instead of
the stretch so he thinks we're ignoring him. Then
I'll pitch out. Down 6–0 he's not gonna run, but you
can pick him off first."

That's what happens with my creativity when I
lose my game face. Sosh looked at me like I was
crazy. "Forget that. Let's get this hitter out."

Sosh headed back to the plate. I turned to Woodson. "What'd you think?"

"I liked it."

"Me too," I said. "Who died and left him captain?"

Howard Johnson was at the plate and the crowd
noise rose again. As if I needed the message one
more time, I had discovered the importance of one
pitch. I would have time later to enjoy, to celebrate,
to take it all in. I would even have time to thank
God. But all that depended on the next pitch. Without proper execution, there is no result, no celebra-
tion.

I put my game face back on, zoned out everything
else, and might as well have been in an exhibition
game. I was still juiced up by the crowd as I got two
strikes on Johnson, but I forced myself to channel
that emotion and that adrenalin. We had worked
Johnson with curves most of the Series, so we went
to a fastball. The called third strike brought us what
we had been working toward all year. We had won,
and the place went nuts. I quickly dropped to one
knee and breathed a prayer of thanks, rising just in
time to be mobbed by my teammates.

The clubhouse was more like a madhouse after
that one. Mickey Hatcher wore goggles. Tommy
kept screaming his love to everyone. He asked
Mickey, "Have I told you that I love you?"

"Not in the last five seconds," Hatch said.

Tommy grabbed me away from an interview, tearing the earphones off my head. "Get over here and celebrate with your teammates!" he shouted. He didn't know I was trying to give them the credit for my having been named Most Valuable Player in the National League Championship Series.

Tommy kept shouting, "No one believed we could beat the mighty Mets! This is the biggest win of our lives!" He told anybody who would listen that this was the best team he ever had, not because of talent because we certainly weren't the most talented he'd ever had. "Because of their heart," he would say. "They never gave up, never gave in, defied all the odds. This was the most satisfying." I couldn't quit grinning. What a way to win a trip to the Series!

When Tommy finally settled down, he was more reflective. "We kept hearing about the Mets, how they led the league in homers, in ERA, in extra-base hits, all that. And there's no question, they *are* the best all-around team in the league. It was hard to imagine, especially with what everybody was saying, that we even belonged on the same field with them. During the regular season, in ten of eleven games, we apparently *didn't*.

"But once again this proves that it's not always the strongest one who wins the fight, or the fastest man who wins the race, or the best team who wins the game. It's the one who wants it just a little bit more."

Dwight Gooden said that when the Mets had beat us the night before, "I thought sure we'd win tonight. But they were aggressive. I have to give them that."

Tommy had the last word. "I love these guys! They're a team of destiny!"

I wasn't so sure about that. I didn't want people thinking that because we were a team of destiny, all we had to do was show up and throw our gloves out there and we would win. That series was hard-fought, and now we had to face Oakland. Talk about mighty! This was a team that scored nearly a hundred runs more than the Mets during the year, a team that won 104 games, a team with power hitters to spare—Dave Parker, Mark McGwire, and the unbelievable José Canseco.

Three days later we would host Oakland in the opener, and all the talk would be just that. The winner would have to be determined on the field.

We were more concerned about Kirk Gibson's severely sprained knee than we were about the experts saying we had no business in the Series. Gibby's knee, combined with his hamstring injuries, made it almost impossible for him to walk, let alone run or swing a bat properly. It was tough enough to have gone through most of the season and the playoffs without Fernando. Marshall's back was still acting up, and the rest of us had the usual list of nagging injuries we wouldn't even discuss.

It was going to be an uphill battle; we knew that. Tim Belcher was to start in the opener. I was scheduled for game two. The three days between the end of the playoffs and the start of the World Series were the longest wait of the year. We had heard enough and read enough and said enough. We wanted to quit listening, reading, and talking, and start playing.

20

MIRACLE FINISH

Steve Boros, Jerry Stephenson, and Mel Didier are names seldom associated with the Dodgers, but they proved as important as anyone on the field—especially in the first game of the Series. They are our scouts, the men who watched the Oakland A's at the end of the season and in the American League Championship Series.

They were the ones who provided the information for our pre-game meeting about what each hitter liked and didn't like, who was hot, who was dangerous. An example: "Stay low on [Dave] Parker. Don't let [José] Canseco get his arms extended, but make sure the inside fastball really jams him." The scouting report also tried to help our hitters, telling them what certain pitchers like to throw in specific situations. "[Dennis] Eckersley sometimes throws a backdoor slider to a left-handed hitter with a 3–2 count."

The hoopla surrounding the World Series can be great fun, but it can also be a distraction. It seems the locker room is always full of strangers, the field is swarming with reporters, and anything anyone suspects might be interesting to anyone else becomes big news. Gibby grew irritated at having to report on the condition of his legs every few minutes. Finally he told everybody that if he played, he would be at sixty or seventy percent, and that it would be up to Tommy if he thought that was enough.

By game time, however, Gibby had admitted privately to Tommy that he had nothing to offer. He could barely move, he couldn't run, and he couldn't shift his weight in the batter's box to drive off either leg. He wouldn't even be coming out for the introductions, so he didn't even dress for the game. Tommy penciled Mickey Hatcher into left field, batting third, and Gibby watched the game first from the training room and eventually from the TV room.

I joined him there after a few outs. Though I was starting the next day and was allowed to go home after the second inning, I wanted to watch the A's hit during the whole game. I hadn't faced these guys before, and though we had gone over the scouting report the night before and during the pre-game meeting, there's nothing like seeing a team for yourself. Anyway, who leaves a World Series game after the second inning?

What Gibby and I saw was not pretty. Belcher was rocky in the first inning after striking out leadoff man Carney Lansford. Dave Henderson singled to center, Canseco was hit by a pitch, and after Parker flied out to center, McGwire walked. The bases were loaded and there were two outs. Timmy escaped by getting Terry Steinbach to fly out to center, and we all breathed easier. In the top of the second, he would face the bottom of the A's order. That had to be easier.

In the bottom of the first, Saxy got us started again. He was hit by a Dave Stewart pitch and moved to second on a balk. After Stubbs flied out to center, Hatcher did what Kirk Gibson's replacement should do and drilled an 0–1 pitch 375 feet over the left field wall to give us a 2–0 lead. It was great fun to watch Hatch sprint around the bases. He wasn't trying to show up anyone he explained later, "I just haven't ever had to develop a home run trot."

In the top of the second, Oakland second baseman Glenn Hubbard led off with a single to left. Walt Weiss struck out, but Stewart walked. Walks have a way of hurting you. Walking the pitcher has a way of killing you. Clearly Timmy was frustrated with Hubbard at second and the pitcher at first. When he walked Lansford, the A's had the bases loaded and only one out. The big hitters were just around the corner. After Henderson came Canseco, Parker, and McGwire. Timmy got Henderson on strikes. Now if he could just get Canseco.

José would later be named the Most Valuable Player in the American League. He had been the first player in history to steal 40 bases and hit 40 home runs in one season. More impressive, he had predicted it before the year began.

When Timmy fell behind 1–0, Canseco looked for his pitch. Four hundred feet later, the ball and our lead landed beyond the center field wall. His grand slam made it 4–2 A's. We couldn't know it would be Canseco's last hit of the entire Series and the A's last runs in the game. The question now was whether we could come back.

Or was this just a foretaste of those legendary Bash Brothers? Would those guys be doing this to us every game, letting us get a few runs and then smothering us? Leary, Holton, and Peña combined to hold the A's scoreless the rest of the game, but Stewart settled down after his shaky first inning, too. Alfredo Griffin managed a two-out single to right in the second, then Stewart allowed only a pair of walks before the sixth.

With one out, Marshall, Hatcher, and Scioscia touched Stewart for a run on three straight singles, one to right, one to center, and one to left. We trailed 4-3 going into the last third of the game, but Stewart was stingy.

In the seventh Sax reached second on a single and a steal with two outs, but died there. By now Gibson and I were in the TV room, wondering if there was hope. When Dodger announcer Vin Scully looked ahead and tried to list the possible pinch hitters against Oakland relief ace Dennis Eckersley, should he be called upon to shut us down in the eighth or ninth, Scully said something about Gibson not being available. Kirk stood painfully and began pacing.

"Who says I can't hit? I might be able to hit."

I glanced up at him. He had that on-edge look. Maybe he could hit, but he sure was having trouble walking. He couldn't favor one leg because both were equally painful. Yet I had seen him play on hamstrings that should have shut him down. He just goes out there and grits it out.

Gibby limped to the training room and plopped ice

bags on his legs. "I'm gonna see if I can do it," he told
Dr. Bill [Buhler, our head trainer].

While in the eighth, Hatcher, Marshall, and
Shelby were going down in order, Gibby was getting
dressed and heading for the batting cage in the
tunnel. He had a bat boy set balls up on the tee while
he practiced his swing. He looked terrible, wincing
with every move. "Can you hit?" I asked. "What do
you think?" He opened his hips, shifted his weight,
and took an awkward slap at the ball. "Yeah, why
not?"

Meanwhile, Alejandro Peña held off the A's in the
top of the ninth, despite a two-out infield single by
Stan Javier. Gibby sent the bat boy for Tommy, who
came jogging through the tunnel. I went into the
dugout to watch the rest of the game from there.

Tommy Lasorda picks up the story: "Gibson
couldn't do anything, everybody knew that—me, the
A's, the TV people. He had told me, 'There isn't
anything I can do for you.' So that's the way we
played the game, knowing that. Then when we came
to bat in the bottom of the ninth, our sixth, seventh,
and eighth hitters were due up—Scioscia, Hamilton,
and Griffin. I was gonna have Mike Davis hit for
Peña, the ninth hitter, in case anybody got on.

"Just as we're comin' off the field, the bat boy
comes to me and says, 'Gibson wants to see you in
the runway.' I run up there, havin' no idea what he
wants, and he says, 'I think I can hit for you.' I say,
'Great,' and I run back to the dugout and change it.
I tell Davis to hit for Griffin. Now if any of the three
of 'em get on, I'm goin' with Gibson."

The A's brought in their ace, Dennis Eckersley, a
dominant stopper, possibly the best in baseball in

1988. After Scioscia popped out to second to lead off the bottom of the ninth, he sat next to me. Hamilton quickly fell behind in the count. When he struck out, the crowd was silent and Mike Davis headed for the plate. Gibson was in the dugout now, but Tommy was hiding him in the corner. "Guess who's gonna hit if Davis gets on?" I asked Sosh.

He shrugged. "Dempsey or Anderson, I guess. There goes Anderson."

"Nope."

"He's on deck."

"Nope. Gibby."

He looked hard at me. "Gibby can't hit. He can't even walk."

"I just saw him hitting off the tee in the tunnel, and he says he can."

Tommy: "When Davis goes in to hit for Griffin, Gibson wants to go out on deck, but I tell him, 'No, you stay behind me here in the corner.' I send Anderson out, who hasn't played for two months and wasn't even on the list for the playoffs. When I saw [A's catcher Ron] Hassey go to the mound and then him and Eck take a peek at Anderson on deck, I know this is workin'. No way they're gonna let a pretty good long ball hitter like Davis beat 'em if they can be careful with him and still pitch to Anderson. Davis hadn't had much of a year with us, but he had been with the A's the year before and hit over 20 home runs. They knew him all right."

Millions watching on television heard NBC's play-by-play man, Vin Scully, say, ". . . and he walked him."

When Davis walked on five pitches, Tommy called Anderson back and pushed Gibby out of the dugout. "Now go get 'em," he said. The place went nuts. Sosh and I were excited again. Gibson had been our hero all year, had done so many amazing clutch things for us. Maybe we still had a chance. All we needed was a run to tie, but with two out and Eckersley on the mound . . .

Scully continued: "All year long they looked to him to light the fire, and all year long he answered the demands, until he was physically unable to start tonight with two bad legs."

When Gibby fouled off the first pitch, he looked terrible. He almost fell over. Our hopes turned to disgust. There was no way he was going to come through now. I said, "Tommy's got to get him out of there. He doesn't have a chance. He's got to get him out."

Scully: "With two out, you talk about a roll of the dice, this is it."

Tommy: "I knew one thing: that we could steal on Eckersley. Davis is the tying run, and I say to myself, 'I give Gibson two shots to hit the ball out of the park. If he doesn't do it, with two strikes I'll send Davis."

Gibson fouled off another and it was 0–2. He looked as if he could hardly stand up out there. We hoped Davis would steal and leave first base open. Maybe the A's would be foolish enough to walk Gibson and give Sax a chance. That was our only prayer.

Scully: "Sax waiting on deck, but the game right now is at the plate."

When Davis didn't steal, the guys on the bench were looking at each other, wondering when he would be sent. It was clear to everyone that the only thing Gibson could do was maybe flare a hit over the infield, but that wouldn't score Davis from first.

When Gibson squibbed the next pitch down the first base line and started hobbling toward first, I was sure the game was over. But the ball rolled foul. Gibby limped back to the plate. Davis had been moving on the pitch. He was going on the next one too, but Gibby fouled it back again. Davis had the base stolen standing up, but Gibby had to swing. No way he could let a close pitch go by now.

The next pitch was outside. Davis stole second without drawing a throw. Now we had a chance. Gibson would no longer have to hit a dinger. (Tommy says he can't hit one out when he tries anyway; he hits his home runs when he's just trying to make contact.) All we needed was a base hit, and Davis would never stop running.

Ball two, 2–2.

Ball three, 3–2.

Maybe it could have been more dramatic. Down 4–3, bottom of the ninth, runner on second, first game of the World Series, the hitter is the team's hero, but he's limped to the plate. Sosh and I sat there rooting not for a homer or even a line drive. Just a bleeder, even a walk. Give Saxy a chance.

And then Eckersley did just what our scouts said he would do with a left-handed hitter on a 3–2 count. He threw a backdoor slider that was down but over the plate. Gibby swung just to meet it. He lifted a high drive to deep right field. I jumped up to watch Canseco, knowing that if he turned, we had a chance. He was turning! I looked back at Gibby who was watching the ball as he broke from the batter's box.

Scully: "High flyball into right field! She . . . is . . . gone!"

We leaped from the dugout, and I crossed in front of Tommy, who bounded toward the plate, arms raised, shouting "Oh, yeah! Oh, yeah!" I jumped up and down like a little kid. We all did, people in the stands, everyone. Gibby circled the bases gingerly like a newborn deer, shadow boxing the air in triumph, flashing a wide grin.

Scully: "In a year that has been so improbable, the impossible has happened!"

We tried to mob Gibby at the plate, but he pushed us back. "Get away!" he shouted. Our weight would have been too much for his legs. We tried to lift him. "No! Not that either!" The guy was too sore to be congratulated or carried on our shoulders, yet he had volunteered to hit, sacrificing himself for the team. What a gamer!

That was to be Gibson's only plate appearance in the 1988 World Series. There had been seven previous ninth-inning game-winning home runs in Series history, but his was the first in 496 Series games (all of them) that brought a team from behind to victory.

It was the greatest moment in sports I've been involved in where I wasn't playing. I didn't even mind not having participated in that game. It was a privilege even to have been in the ballpark. During rain delays of televised games for the next 25 years, that will be the highlight broadcast to fans all over the country.

I had planned to take home the scouting report and a video of that game so I could study the hitters, make notes, and walk myself through the sequences I might try as the starter in game two. But Gibby's home run was so exciting that I forgot all about it, showered, and went straight home.

I had to come to the stadium early the next day and cram. Fearing I would mix up one hitter for another, I made myself a cheat sheet. Before the game I would have to show the umpires what I might pull out of my back pocket during the game. I didn't know if it would help, but I sure felt better with it on me.

21

WORLD BEATERS

Three days before game two my parents called to tell me they had been asked to throw out the first ball, but they wanted to be sure it was all right with me. "This is your night, not ours, and we don't want to do anything that would upset your preparation." That's just an example of the type of concern they have for their kids, always putting us ahead of themselves. Of course, I was thrilled and insisted that they do it.

They had been named Little League Parents of the Year. Believe me, they were not chosen simply because I'm a big leaguer. They truly gave themselves to Little League for years. Dad coached and umpired and Mom ran the concession stand. I remember many a summer evening dinner at the field. Before the game I couldn't really concentrate and get on my game face until I had greeted my mom. After Dad had pitched one to Sosh and Mom to Dempsey, Demper told me, "I can see where you get your ability. Your mom's got good stuff."

Having her and Dad there must have inspired me.

The game had to be one of the highlights of my baseball career. If the night before had been exciting to watch, this one was incredible to play in. Here's just an overview of the highlights:

I shut out the A's on three hits, all singles, and all by Dave Parker.

I faced the minimum number of hitters in the first six innings, getting Mark McGwire to hit into double plays after each of Parker's first two singles. After having struck out the last hitter in the third, I struck out the side in the fourth for four straight strikeouts (I finished with eight). In the ninth I struck out Parker on a low, inside curveball to end the game with a runner in scoring position.

I went three-for-three at the plate with two doubles and an RBI, getting as many hits as the A's and more total bases. I became the first pitcher to go three-for-three in a Series since Art Nehf of the New York Giants did it against the Washington Senators in 1924. (The last pitcher to get three hits in an entire Series was Detroit Tiger Mickey Lolich, who won three games against the Cardinals in 1968.) Because my next appearance would be in the American League park and we used designated hitters for the pitchers, that three-for-three would remain my mark for the 1988 Series.

My first at-bat came in the bottom of the third with one out, none on, and no score. I singled up the middle, then got a good jump and came all the way around to third on Sax's single to right. I scored on Stubbs's single to right, and Sax scored on Hatcher's single to center. Marshall made it 5–0 with a three-run homer to left on a two-strike fastball. Mike said later he knew that with me on the mound, Oakland pitcher Storm Davis needed a strikeout, so Mike sat on the inside fastball. His homer to the left field pavilion was our fifth straight hit (one short of the record set by the Cubs in 1908), and at 5–0 I had more than enough of a cushion.

We scored one more in the fourth when I faked a bunt with Griffin on first (after a one-out single) and slapped a double down the right field line. Alfredo scored all the way from first. I also doubled in the sixth and was our last base runner.

I may have pitched better games, though allowing only three hits and walking just two made it one of my best. But putting the offense and the pitching together, I'd have to say it was the game of a lifetime. It was our third straight win and my second straight post-season shut out and gave me 93⅓ innings in which I had allowed a total of three earned runs.

I know my hits were a gift. I love to hit, but I have to credit a little luck when I go three-for-three. A pitcher will never hit well for a season, even if he takes daily batting practice. Hitting ninth, he will come to the plate only three times in a game, provided he pitches well enough to stay in that long. Two of those three times he might be asked to bunt. There's nothing like facing live pitching to perfect your timing, which is impossible when you play only once every four or five days. That's why the good-hitting pitcher is such a rarity.

The next three games, the first coming two days later, would be at Oakland. Much as we loved playing in Dodger Stadium at Chavez Ravine, our goal was to finish this thing in Oakland. If we went back to Chavez, that meant the A's would win two of the next three. If we beat them to it, it would be all over.

It was John Tudor against former Dodger Bob Welch in game three, and both started strong. After giving up a single to right by Sax, Welch struck out the side in the first and two more in the second, though he allowed a single and a walk. Tudor retired the side in order in the first and struck out McGwire to lead off the bottom of the second, then left the mound with an elbow injury. Tim Leary came in to relieve. It was the last we would see of Tudor in the Series. No Tudor. No Gibson. Marshall's hurting. Though we led by two games, my gut told me we were in trouble.

While Welch got us out in order in the top of the third, the A's pushed ahead in the bottom half. Glenn Hubbard singled to left, stole second, and advanced to third on Sosh's throwing error. Ron Hassey drove him in with another single to left before Leary shut them down. We tied the game 1-1 in the fifth after Hamilton led off with a single to center, was sacrificed to second by Griffin, and scored on Stubbs's double to right center.

Leary allowed the A's only one more hit before being lifted after the fifth. Peña came on to pitch one-hit, shut out ball for the next three innings.

The top of the sixth proved to be as frustrating as any half inning all year. Danny Heep led off with a double to left that Luis Polonia probably should have caught. Shelby singled to left, and Polonia, for some reason, threw home. That allowed Shelby to advance to second. Two on, none out. When Davis walked, everybody in the park figured we'd be up by at least two by the time the half inning was over. Oakland manager Tony LaRussa went to left-handed reliever Greg Cadaret. Down two games to none, he had to try everything to keep us from going ahead.

Normally, Tommy would have countered by removing Sosh and having Dempsey face the left-hander, but Heep had already substituted for Mike Marshall, who was hurt, and Tracy Woodson would replace Stubbs when the A's went to their right-handed relievers. Tommy couldn't afford to run out of pinch hitters.

Sosh fouled out on a 0–1 pitch, and LaRussa went to right-hand reliever Gene Nelson. Hamilton grounded a 0–1 pitch to third, and Lansford threw home for the force. Two out. Griffin grounded out on the first pitch, and suddenly we had gone from bases loaded with no outs to a scoreless inning in just five pitches. The A's were as pumped as we were flat.

We managed only a two-out single from Hatcher in the seventh after that. Tommy brought in Jay Howell for the bottom of the ninth. We were tied 1–1. Jay got Canseco to pop out to second, then went to 3–2 on McGwire. The big man blasted the next pitch 375 feet to left for the game-winning homer, and it was over. Just like that.

I met Jay near the first baseline as he trudged off the field. "Did you make a good pitch?"

He nodded, eyes down, lips pressed tight.

"Then you gave it your best shot. We'll get 'em tomorrow."

At times like those, it doesn't do any good to hang your head and get upset. If you get beat, learn from it. If it was your best pitch, that's all you can ask. If it wasn't, don't throw it again. Neither of us knew it, of course, but the next night Jay would get a chance to redeem himself by facing the heart of the Oakland batting order twice with a one-run lead.

The A's had produced just six runs in three games, five from two home runs. And though we appeared to have dominated them, they trailed in games only 2–1 now. The momentum, the home field advantage, and the odds seemed to favor them.

Before game four, a bunch of us were standing around watching the pre-game show on television. I said, "Let's get on the field. We can't win this game in the clubhouse! That TV can't help us." I reached up to turn it off, but Tommy eye-balled me.

"Just a minute, Bulldog. Let's see what [NBC broadcaster Bob] Costas has to say."

Just then, Costas called our lineup "perhaps the weakest in World Series history." He was right, of course. We had been saying the same thing ourselves. Because of all the injuries, we fielded a team that had one hitter with an average of under .100, one under .200, and two others under .240. That lineup accounted for 34 home runs for the year, compared to Canseco's 42, McGwire's 32, and the A's total of 156. But boy, hearing Costas say that on national television really riled us up. Tommy took that comment and ran with it.

"Do you believe that guy?" he said. "Did you hear what he said about us?"

By the time we headed for the field, guys were yelling, "Kill Costas!" Maybe the TV *could* help us win.

It was Belcher against Stewart again, and as he had done so many times during the season, Steve Sax started us off right. He walked and advanced to third when Hatcher singled to right. Sax scored on a passed ball and Hatcher later scored on a fielder's choice. We had produced two runs on one hit and an error.

The A's didn't let us run away with it, breaking back for a run of their own in the bottom of the inning. Luis Polonia singled to left, reached second on a passed ball, advanced to third on a groundout to first, and scored when Canseco grounded out to second. We led 2–1. We added a run in the top of the third when Stubbs doubled to center and scored on an error. In the fourth, Sosh singled to right but severely twisted his knee trying to steal second. He would be out for the rest of the Series. We were down to a few remaining healthy bodies.

Meanwhile, Belcher settled down and allowed only two more hits until the sixth. That's when Dave Henderson doubled to left for the only extra-base hit the Athletics produced all night. It looked like he might be stranded there when Timmy got Canseco on a popout to first and Parker on a flyball to left. But, after McGwire walked, Lansford singled to right, driving in Henderson.

We led 3–2 going into the top of the seventh, when we picked up an insurance run. Griffin drew a one-out walk and Sax singled to center. Griffin scored on a too-late double play attempt to make it 4–2. The A's stayed maddeningly close by scoring again in the bottom of the seventh. Walt Weiss reached on a one-out, infield single and scored on a double by Henderson, his third of four straight hits. We led 4–3.

Tommy brought in Jay Howell (the Rifleman), who walked Canseco and saw Parker reach on an error. We had to wonder if Jay was jinxed, but he pitched his way out of the jam by getting McGwire to pop out. That was a big out for Jay's confidence after having thrown the home run ball to McGwire the night before. He allowed a two-out single to pinch hitter Ron Hassey in the bottom of the eighth, but struck out Weiss to end the threat.

Jay carried the thin 4–3 lead into the bottom of the ninth and had to face the top of the order again. He got Polonia on a fly to left, saw Henderson get his fourth hit (a single to left), then struck out Canseco. When Parker popped out to third, we had won.

That was one hard-fought victory. Both teams played well, but the A's could see their hopes fading. Canseco, Parker, and McGwire had gone 0 for 11, and it was clear the snake-bit Athletics had to get run-production out of them if they hoped to stay alive in the Series.

Of course, I hoped to end it with a fifth game victory the next night, but I had to wonder if that was too much to ask. It wasn't as if I hadn't had any breaks in 1988. Winning the division was almost enough for me, but 23 wins was great, too. The scoreless inning streak was icing on the cake. I was thrilled that we beat the Mets, and being the playoff MVP moved my year past fantastic and close to ridiculous.

Shutting out the Mets to end it, well . . . I had worked hard and it wasn't much fun (until that last inning when I tried to enjoy it and plunked Mazzilli), so I resented it a little when people started saying I was on a magic carpet or that I was living a charmed life. I felt charmed all right, but this was pressure. I knew I would enjoy it when it was over, but I also wanted one more good performance. I believe in the probabilities of baseball, but I didn't see any reason why the law of averages should catch up to me and make me a different pitcher than I had been since late August. I appreciated former slugger Reggie Jackson's comment about me before the game. He said I was "the real thing. He's 24 carat. He's 99 and 44/100 percent pure. He's Ivory Snow. He's Post Toasties. He's a rainy day for the other team. He's a smog alert."

For the fourth time in five games, we scored first (in the first inning for the third time in the Series). Stubbs singled to right with one out and Hatcher hit his second homer of the season, 360 feet to left.

I retired the first six hitters I faced, and leading 2–0 going into the bottom of the third, I allowed my first run in more than 21 innings. Lansford and Tony Phillips hit back to back singles to lead off, moved up on a sacrifice bunt by Weiss, and Lansford scored on Javier's sacrifice fly. We led 2–1.

In the top of the fourth, we added some insurance. Hatcher led off with a single, and after two straight strikeouts, Mike Davis came to the plate. Mike's a good friend who had suffered in a reserve role all season. He had been brought over from the A's to play the outfield, but when Moose's bad back made it impossible for him to play first, Moose moved into Mike's position.

Because he was such a great competitor and a real professional, it was hard for Mike to ride the bench. He hit .196 and had just two homers for the year. At times he wondered if he should ask to be traded. We prayed about it together, and I tried to encourage him. "If God doesn't want you here, a trade will come up naturally. You'll get moved. But I don't think it's clear that you're not supposed to be here. Let's hang in and have patience and wait on God." I didn't want him to leave the ballclub. He was one of the most spiritual Christians around, a guy who could fill in for the chapel leader any time and have something meaningful to say from Scripture.

As the year went on, I became convinced that if Mike maintained a good attitude, God would lift him up and he would shine in the end. "He's going to reward you for your patience, for being good and not becoming a team problem. If somebody gets hurt, you're going to fill in. You're going to do something good, maybe even be the World Series MVP."

Down 2–1 with two out and Hatcher on first, Storm Davis ran the count to 3–0 on Mike. Then Tommy took a chance. He gave Mike the hit sign.

Tommy: "We weren't scoring enough runs. We had a team out there that was nowhere near our regular ballclub. I knew one thing: if I'm the pitcher in that situation, I gotta throw a strike. I'm not gonna throw my best fastball over the plate. If this guy's gonna hit one out on me, he's gonna hafta do it all on his own off a mediocre fastball. And that's just what Davis did."

Mike drove the ball 360 feet to right for a two-run homer and a 4–1 lead. I was the first to greet him at the plate. I smacked his hands and held on as we stared at each other. "Praise God!" I said. "I knew you'd come through!"

"Yes," Mike said. "Praise God! Praise God!"

That lead was a real confidence-builder for me. Clearly I had been in a groove for weeks, but when you add a margin like that to a pitcher whose stuff is working, he's hard to beat.

As we moved closer and closer to the end of the game and the end of the Series, the crowd noise washed over us like waves. I began keeping myself relaxed by yawning, praying, talking to myself, and singing. The TV cameras caught me in the dugout more than once with my head back, singing softly. I was singing hymns, but no one knew that.

We scratched out a fifth run in the top of the sixth when Davis walked with two out and scored on a double by Demper. In the bottom of the inning, up 5–1, retired the side in order on 11 pitches, yet I left the mound like an intense soldier and came to the dugout mad. I threw my glove against the wall, slammed my hat on the bench, grabbed my jacket and stomped to the water cooler. People who saw it on TV wondered if I had been told I was coming out. My teammates thought I was crazy. The problem was that I wasn't mentally in the game, despite my success that half inning. In my mind, I had pitched poorly. I hadn't had the intensity. I wasn't executing the pitches the way I should, and I knew I would not get away with that for long. I needed to wake myself up and get back in the game. Silently I berated myself, "You've got to be better, now come on!"

My teammates said, "Cool down, man. It's gonna be OK. Three up three down we can live with."

When I faced Tony Phillips to lead off the eighth, I hadn't allowed a base runner since giving up a two-out walk in the fourth. The A's were trying to get to me and interrupt my rhythm by stepping out of the box at the last minute, after I had started my delivery. Plate umpire Jerry Crawford would raise his hand and call time, signaling no pitch. I didn't want to be nasty, but I thought that was pretty cheap. When Phillips did it to me a couple of times in a row, I moved toward the plate and hollered at Crawford loud enough for Phillips to hear. "How late can they step out on me before it's a problem?"

"You know they can step out for a lot of reasons," he said.

"Well, you can just tell 'em it only makes me more aggressive. I only want to get 'em out even more." And I turned back to the mound. Their technique was going to backfire if I had my way, because I had learned to channel the adrenalin caused by that irritation. If it bothered me, it only made me more intense.

I walked Phillips, and one out later, Javier singled to center on the first pitch, scoring Phillips from second. Our lead was cut to 5–2. With the Oakland fans chanting "Or-el! Or-el!" in the taunting, demeaning way a lot of crowds do to Strawberry ("Dar-ryl! Dar-ryl!") and other stars, I walked Henderson on four pitches, then wild pitched both runners up a base.

The bullpen was up and working. Leading by three with runners at second and third, one out, and Canseco representing the tying run, Tommy admitted later he thought I'd lost my effectiveness. Though Canseco was one for 18 in the Series to that point, he was still dangerous. His only hit had been the grand slam in game one, and another shot like that would tie this one. The Oakland fans were delirious.

I worked Canseco carefully, and when I got him to 1–2, Demper jogged out to the mound, having detected something. "I think he's looking for a ball out over the plate. Get it in on him. Jam him." I threw him an inside fastball for the only time in the Series. He's so strong I knew I could get away with that only if I surprised him. He popped out to first for the second out, and here came Parker.

Dave is a confident hitter. He owned me in game two (getting all three of Oakland's hits). I had lockered next to him on a team in Venezuela during winter ball several years before. He's one huge guy, an intense competitor, very good at what he does—and that's hit.

I'd had good luck with him all night, getting him three times in the infield. I got ahead of him 1–2 on a 55-foot curve, so I came back with the same pitch and struck him out. After the way he's hit me over the years, he owed me that one.

We had managed only a walk in the last three innings ourselves. Since my eighth-inning performance had been sub-par, some may have wondered if I had enough left to finish off the A's. I was confident. In my mind, the game had ridden on the Canseco and Parker at-bats in the eighth. Before the bottom of the ninth I uncharacteristically flashed three fingers at the camera in the dugout and mouthed, "Three more outs." Normally I'm not an out counter, but I could taste the world's championship. In the stands my father had held up six fingers before the eighth. Jamie, next to him, didn't like that. She was afraid of the embarrassment if it backfired. If it wasn't bad luck, it bordered on cockiness or poor sportsmanship. Obviously, Dad didn't mean it that way. He was just hoping, encouraging, urging me on. The second time he did it,

Jamie asked him not to, assuring him that I would never do that. She was stunned later to find out that I had.

I couldn't wait to get out there for the bottom of the ninth. I knew the country was watching on television, but what made it so special was how underrated we had been. No one had given us a prayer against the Mets, and when we supposedly lucked our way to a narrow 4–3 margin over them, we were expected to be a piece of cake for the Athletics.

Our team was the walking wounded. Mickey Hatcher's Stuntmen, led by Mickey himself, stepped forward as they had all season and did the job. This victory would be for them. For Tommy the Motivator. For Gibby the Martyr who had sacrificed himself all year. For Fernando who had to sit and watch, and for all the others who had invested their bodies in the cause.

We weren't the best team in the major leagues. We were simply about to become the world champs. We had wanted it, worked for it, and believed we could do it. No one had been afraid to play, to take risks, to pay the price. This was going to be sweet.

I didn't want to make the same mistake I had made in the ninth inning of the last game against the Mets. I didn't want to get too far out of my zone, too far from my game face before we had really tucked it away. Three runs against a team like Oakland might mean about as much as two runs had to the Mets in the first game of the playoffs: simply a target.

Big Mark McGwire led off. He and Canseco had suffered through the Series with a homer each for their only hits. If anything, that made him all the more dangerous. He crushed a 1–1 pitch to deep center, and I was relieved when Shelby caught it at the base of the wall. Two outs to go.

I went quickly to 0–2 on Hassey then caught him looking at a breaking ball for my eighth strikeout. It was hard to contain the grin now. I wanted to savor this, to enjoy it. But I had work to do. One out to go.

Carney Lansford had singled and scored a run, and twice flied out to center. Now he hit a shot into the hole between third and short, and Alfredo had to race almost to the foul line to backhand it. He tried a long, off-balance throw and almost got Lansford at first. It was only the fourth hit I had given up.

With a runner on, the A's fans still believed. The noise was deafening, taking on a personality of its own. When Tony Phillips came to the plate, Terry Steinbach moved to the on-deck circle, prepared to hit for Walt Weiss. I wanted to end it right then so I wouldn't have to face the tying run. I decided to ignore the runner and pitch from a wind up. Phillips had singled, struck out, walked, set up one run, and scored another. I overthrew and started him off with a ball. Lansford realized we weren't even paying attention to him, so he stole second on the next pitch without drawing a throw. Ball two.

All I cared about was making sure Steinbach didn't get to the plate. I had seen him homer in the all-star game. He was capable of anything. On ball three, Lansford moved to third. I had struggled in the eighth, and now I was really in trouble in the ninth. I took my time and regrouped.

I worked back up to a full count, with Phillips taking all the way. Lansford edged up the line from third. I wound and fired. He swung. Strike three!

Vin Scully said that like the 1969 Mets, it was the impossible dream revisited. There was no time to kneel, but I raised my eyes and sneaked in a prayer of thanks. We had done it. We had won the World Series.

The number two through six hitters for the A's had gone 0 for 17 in the game, and a sportswriter said Oakland should change its name from the A's to the F's, because they had failed their Orel exam. They had hit .177 in the Series and scored 11 runs in five games. I won't take anything away from the A's though. Their regular season record and their playoff rout of the Red Sox speaks for itself. They hit a slump while we were hot, and that was the story of the 1988 Series.

I was upset with myself because my game face was still on when we celebrated after the final out. I was smiling, but I was still tight. I had not let go, not let it sink in. As I neared the dugout I searched for Jamie in the stands. When I found her waving and cheering for me, I raised both fists and let it out. The grin came. Winning it all was almost too much to believe, but sharing it with her made the moment perfect.

In the locker room I was informed that I had been named player of the game and MVP for the Series. Bob Costas of NBC interviewed me on nationwide television. I told him I had struggled several times, and explained that I had switched to lots of change ups and off-speed pitches once we got the big lead. "That got me into trouble, because when I went back to the hard stuff, it was a different energy level and I found it tough to keep the fastball from sailing."

Costas asked me what I was doing between innings when the cameras had caught me in the dugout with my head back, "eyes closed, almost meditating."

"I was singing hymns to myself to relax and keep my adrenalin down, because every time I thought about being ahead, I got too excited to pitch."

"How can you be so composed after a season like this and a playoff and World Series performance like this that has, it's fair to say, etched you a spot eternally in baseball lore?"

"Well, I feel that the Lord has blessed me with composure and has kept me calm through the whole thing. I know this isn't a religious show, but I just thank God for everything that's happened this year for our ballclub. . . ."

". . . Are you going to be called up to a higher league? You're too good for these guys!"

"No. I feel like I'm climbing a mountain every time out there. It is really hard to pitch in the big leagues, believe me. It's a war out there."

When I got off the raised platform with Costas, a representative of the Baseball Hall of Fame introduced himself and said, "Orel, we'd like to have your jersey for Cooperstown, because you were the Series MVP." I was beside myself. I would have given them anything they wanted. Who would have ever dreamed they would want something of mine?

With a crush of reporters around me I made my way to my locker and changed into a dry tee shirt and jacket. I answered questions for another 10 or 15 minutes, my game face returning when I was reminded of the various pressure situations. There was another whole group of media people waiting in an interview room, so as I headed there with a group of reporters, we passed a roped-off area where fans watched us walk by. Out of the crowd came the piercing voice of a boy about 10:

"You were lucky, Hershiser!"

I stopped and stared at him there, an arrogant look under an Oakland cap.

"Grab a bat, kid," I said.

The boy looked thrilled that he had gotten my attention. I didn't smile until I was out of his field of vision, then I grinned at one of the reporters.

Later, when I was finally able to get to the A's clubhouse, I was reminded how we felt in 1985 when we had lost the National League Championship Series to St. Louis. You're down, and yet you had a great year. It's a tough time for intense competitors.

I talked to several of the players, then went to Tony LaRussa's office. He told me, "You were outstanding. It was almost a pleasure to watch you."

I told him I admired his ballclub, and he tipped his hat to me.

José Canseco told a reporter, "I got a dose of [Hershiser's] curveball, which is in Bert Blyleven's class. Great stuff. Great *pitcher*."

My teammates were just as kind. Mickey Hatcher said, "What Orel did at the end of the year was really unbelievable. It's something I'll never forget."

Kirk Gibson said, "I don't know if we will ever again see the likes of what [Orel has] done. It may be that no other pitcher has ever stayed in that kind of groove so long. . . . He'll go down in history."

The duration of that groove *was* stunning, especially to me. When I looked back on the last 101⅓ innings I pitched in 1988 and realize that 96 of them were scoreless, all I can do is shake my head. That's an incomprehensible ERA of 0.62! Of all the pitchers in history who might have enjoyed that kind of a stretch, I can still hardly believe it happened to me.

The next night I was a guest on "The Tonight Show," and my family and several of the Dodgers were in the audience. In Johnny Carson's monologue he said I did so much for the team that not only had I pitched the final game, but I had also caught!

He asked about singing to myself. I tried to downplay it, but he wouldn't have it.

"Do you just hum, or what?" I laughed. "Do you sing?"

"I sing."

The audience clapped and cheered. I hadn't meant *that!*

"I'm not gonna sing!"

They roared.

"Yes you are!" Carson said. "Oh, yes you are!"

I shook my head, panicking. I'd never sung alone in public in my life.

"This could be a first," he pressed. "Just a couple of bars."

The audience would not let up, and I could see there was no way out of it.

"Well, the one I can remember singing the most was just a praise hymn." [Suddenly it was deathly silent.] As I sat on the bench I would sing:

Praise God from whom all blessings flow.
Praise Him all creatures here below.
Praise Him above ye heavenly host.
Praise Father, Son, and Holy Ghost.

Amen.

PART SIX

1989

22

THE TEST

There's nothing like a tough year to test the lofty theories that sounded so good during a miracle season!

During the off-season I became the highest paid player in baseball, more of a national personality because of my endorsements, and was overwhelmed by so many honors and awards that I had to keep pinching myself to be sure I wasn't dreaming. Part of any professional athlete is a confidence that says, "Yeah, I did that," but with most of us—at least speaking for me—there's that part of me that says, "Do you believe this is happening?" I have worked hard and I always aim at achieving at the highest level possible, but frankly, it is still hard to believe what happened in 1988.

I know it's hard to imagine that going from being a Los Angeles celebrity to a national one could present major problems, but it's true. I'd love to be able to stroll in public with my family, go where I want, do what I want without being surrounded. Sure, it's great to be recognized and appreciated and thanked, but I still see myself as just plain, small-town Orel Hershiser. I'm glad to give fans a good experience meeting a big leaguer, but my privacy and anonymity are gone. I miss them. Maybe I'll miss the recognition and attention when I leave the game, but I confess there are times when that seems welcome.

I appeared on a lot of national television commercials and traveled more than I ever have. It was fun, but it puts a lot of pressure on a young family. That's one of the prices you pay for success, and I realize that many people would love to have had my problem. Even when the team went to spring training for the 1989 season, I was determined to keep my mind on the game despite the distractions, and I was glad to get back to the business of baseball. I immediately wished I had become the *second* highest paid player in baseball. It would have been nice for someone else to take some of the media attention. Everything that came my way, all the recognition and fame, set me up for colossal failure. How could I do anything but win twenty games and still be considered a success?

We had a better team than in 1988, but it was a different team. We had lost Steve Sax to the Yankees, getting New York's Willie Randolph in exchange. To our power hitters Gibson, Marshall, and Shelby, we had added American League superstar veteran Eddie Murray. We appeared to have more depth and power, but again, the chemistry would be different. And not everyone would remain healthy.

Sax had given us speed and contagious enthusiasm at the top of the line-up. Randolph and Sax, both great second basemen, are completely different players. Both are assets to ball clubs in their own ways, but you can't ask one to do what the other does. Sax had speed, hit for power, hit in the gaps, was a distraction on the bases, had a sporadic arm, and was average turning the double play.

Willie is a great number-two hitter, a solid team player, good bunter, good hit-and-run man, moves runners along, has below average speed, but turns the double play better than anybody in the big leagues. It's as if the ball hardly touches his glove. He's a great commander and captain, good at positioning the other infielders, and works well with younger players.

The fact is, Sax fit the chemistry of our team better. That sounds like I'm down on Randolph, but I'm not, and he knows I'm not. The Dodgers were unrealistic in hoping Randolph could do what Sax had done. Sax had contagious energy. Willie has the energy but channels it into a quiet professionalism. Sax was more gung-ho, rah-rah, almost hyperactive.

I love Willie Randolph. I think he's fantastic. If we had a leadoff hitter like Rickey Henderson or Willie McGee or Lenny Dykstra, Willie would have been perfect for our team, because he's the perfect second hitter. But don't ask him to lead off when that's not where he belongs. He led off for us for a while, then blossomed in the number-two spot and made the all-star team, so I'm not cutting him down.

Still, I thought we had a better team coming into the season. We had more power, more experience, and post-season play had made us a more mature team. With Gibson, Marshall, and Murray at the center of the line-up, followed by Shelby, Hamilton, and Scioscia, I thought we were deep.

The problem, however, is that we didn't have the leadoff hitter to set the table for the RBI guys. With Sax gone and Gibson still ailing in spring training and for most of the season, we were left without the two fastest guys on our '88 club. The table was not being set with baserunning threats, so there were holes in our line-up.

Gibby tried to play as long as he could, and at 90 percent he's better than most big leaguers. But he wasn't the same player who had been the most valuable Dodger and the most valuable National Leaguer in '88. His injuries were in the legs and they were painful. He couldn't work out as much, so his hitting timing was off too.

Suddenly, team speed was zero.

Opposing pitchers looked at our line-up just like any other and tried to determine who to pitch around and who to go after as pretty sure outs. If our line-up was solid and healthy, we would have been a pitcher's nightmare, like the A's. There was no one to pitch around because the next guy could hurt you. But with Gibson out and Marshall tentative (also due to injuries), Murray didn't see as many hittable pitches. Still he was our top run producer and led the team in RBIs. But one guy can't carry a club offensively. With more bases open, our patched-up line-up was pitched around until the pitchers could get to the tail end of the order.

Meanwhile, Shelby was in the middle of a career-low year. John is a dear friend of mine, and I hope he turns around and has a great big league career. His disappointing season sure wasn't the result of a lack of hard work. He worked his tail off and had faith in himself. He's a positive guy with strong character and a good family. It was just one of those years when a guy struggles at the plate the whole season. A strong example for Christ, John was quiet, solid, not a whiner, and always trying his hardest.

My own season was frustrating too. Going into my first start, the scoreless-inning streak was still alive in the minds of fans and press. In my mind, post-season play (though it didn't count officially as part of the scoreless-inning string) ended the streak, and in exhibition games in Japan I had been shelled. But the streak was still technically alive, and that just added to the publicity pressure.

A flu had kept me from starting the season opener, but I felt ready for game two. The streak ended in the first inning. I erred on a pickoff attempt and Barry Larkin, who had singled, moved to second. Todd Benzinger drove him in with a two-out single between first and second. Despite hitting two singles and pitching fairly well (though inconsistently), I made another error in that game, and Gibson made one. We felt we had given the game away. What a difference a year makes!

I won four of my next five starts, and my other loss was 1–0 in what I considered my best appearance so far. In the game following that one I shut out the Pirates on six hits with no walks and six strike-outs and went to 4–2. I had allowed only one run in 20⅓ innings (ERA 1.58), and our team ERA dropped to 2.34, best in the league. As a team we were 13–13.

With all our changes, injuries, slumps, and frustrations, we never got untracked and never found our rhythm. For a long time I thought we hadn't clicked because we had so many new faces. I thought when Gibby came back, when others got healthy, when slumpers got hot, we'd string together some wins and get right back into the race. When it became obvious we were going to lose Gibson for the year, another element became part of the mix:

Talk.

Everybody was talking, wondering, speculating, looking over their shoulders. Management would have to make a move, wouldn't they? They wouldn't sit on a world's championship and not make a deal when we needed a hitter and an outfielder so badly, would they? But who could we get? And who would be traded? Do we have an expendable pitcher? Will a front-line position player have to be sacrificed?

Names would pop up. What about him? Would the team be better if he was traded for someone to replace Gibson? If you even expressed an opinion, you had taken sides, for or against a teammate, a friend. I tried never to lie. If someone raised the issue and asked what I would think if he was traded, I told the truth. It wasn't easy, but there's no sense lying. I'd say, "I would hate to see you go, because you're a friend and a good guy and you've been good for the Dodgers. And I'd hate to see you have to play with a non-contender. But if we got a power-hitting outfielder in the deal, I'd have to say that if I was the general manager, it's a trade I would make."

Guys appreciated honesty like that. Of course I didn't offer such an opinion unless they asked, but I figured when they asked they wanted some straight talk.

Yet all that talk and speculation distracts a club. Here we're trying to get back on track and all we can talk about is whether a move will be made, and if it's made, who will be involved. In 1988 it seemed all we talked about was how much fun it was to win, how to get a tough hitter out, how many wins we needed on a road trip, ways to polish our fundamentals, anything that would keep us winning.

Now we just wondered and talked and had to work to keep our minds on the game. Trades disrupt lives, especially in the middle of a season. Ballplayers are just like anyone else when it comes to having to move your family, uproot your children, make new friends. No one wants to be traded away from a good organization, a nice park, and a great history, especially coming off a championship season.

The media and the public seemed to say we should forget about the distractions because we were professionals. We were expected to just get out there and play. But we talked about it on the field, in the dugout, in the clubhouse, on the bus, on the plane, and in the hotel. We worried that until a deal was made we would dig ourselves a hole too deep to climb out of. We were losing direction. Such talk starts to break up a team, because rumors rise and fall and players know what each other think about their futures. We wondered and thought and speculated. Meanwhile, we were sinking in the standings. We couldn't get anything going, in spite of good pitching.

By the end of my ninth start I was 6–3, never having gone fewer than seven innings, throwing two shutouts, and losing by just one in two of those losses. The second shutout was a two-hitter against the Phillies, in which I walked four. We finally got out of our own 25-inning scoreless streak and won 9–0.

Seven decisions later I was 9–7, and people who look only at win-loss records wondered what had happened to me. Actually, I was among the league leaders for wins, ERA, shutouts (3), complete games, and strikeouts. We simply weren't winning. Little injuries were decimating our club.

A month to the day after my previous shutout I had beat Houston 3–0. I was flattered that the losing pitcher, Bob Knepper, said later that I was "probably the best right-hander in the National League." The win was our fourth in a row and kept us within five and a half games of the lead. Gibson was leading off temporarily and scored six runs in the four games, including a two-run homer in the shutout.

Eleven days later I threw another shutout, but it was nothing to brag about unless I should be proud of luck. I allowed eleven hits and somehow escaped allowing a run to the Reds. Though we were still in the hunt, seven and a half games out in fourth place, we were a confused ball club.

The team seemed to have no offensive personality. Players wondered whether they were in or out and if they were in, where they would hit. Tommy Lasorda was doing the only thing he knew to do and that was to experiment and find the right combination, the chemistry that would put us on track. But all the uncertainty affected the bench too because the re-serves didn't know their roles from day to day. No one was relaxed about his position, and we were last in the league in batting average and runs scored.

I was honored to be selected for the all-star game, and because Tommy was managing, I volunteered to be his extra-inning insurance. Someone has to fill that role, and it's always a hard choice for an all-star manager. I was glad to help him out, though of course it would have been fun to pitch an inning.

After the break the Dodgers finally made the big trade, sending Tim Leary to Cincinnati for Kal Daniels. Daniels has great power and bad knees, and many wondered about such a risky deal. I'm glad to have him on my side. He had a lifetime .447 average against me and four home runs! I'm confident Kal will become a major contributor to the Dodgers, but by August 7 he was on the fifteen-day disabled list with a sore right knee, and four days later he underwent arthroscopic surgery.

After the all-star break I had the best portion of my season. In my next seven starts I won five (never allowing more than three runs and winning three of those by one run), lost one (2–1), went seven innings and gave up only two runs in a no-decision win, and found myself 14–8.

I fully believed that I had caught fire and that with nine more starts I had the potential to win 20 games and maybe even be in the Cy Young race again. What I didn't know was that I was headed for a nightmare. If anything, those last nine starts were the best part of my season, but in the first eight of those starts I lost seven games and had one no-decision. We scored only five runs and lost five games by one run, including *four* 1–0 shutouts. During that 0–7 string, my ERA was 2.29.

Going into my last start of the season on October 1, I hadn't won since August 8. I was coming off two no-decisions and seven losses, and my record had plummeted to 14–15, though I was second in the league in ERA.

The last loss before that final game was 1–0 to the Padres, and it was gratifying that after the game Tony Gwynn said, "He's pitching as well as he did last year. When anyone looks at his numbers they need to throw out the wins and losses. That low ERA (2.38 at the time and second best in the N.L.) is the most important thing."

Padre manager Jack McKeon said, "You can't take anything away from Hershiser. I don't think we'll ever go through another season and beat him four times again."

For that last start, we traveled to rain-soaked Atlanta for a double-header nobody wanted to play. We were long since out of the running for the pennant, and I simply wanted to avoid a losing season for the first time in my career. I was scheduled to pitch in the second game, but as the rain kept delaying the opener, I had no idea how late that might be. I told Ron Perranoski, "There go our plans. My parents and Jamie and the boys are here and we were going to fly to Florida together tonight."

"Why don't you see if Freddy [Fernando Valenzuela] will trade starts with you," Perry said, "and maybe you can still make your flight."

Freddy agreed immediately, neither of us knowing that the second game was to be canceled anyway. Had he not been so flexible, I would have finished with a losing record. We wondered if even the first game would ever begin, but nearly two and a half hours after the opener was scheduled, we started.

It was ironic that I needed eleven scoreless innings to win the ERA crown when the year before I needed ten in my last start to break the scoreless inning record. Was it possible that I would get to pitch eleven innings, just when I needed it most? I guess I live a charmed life. I pitched eleven innings, but I gave up an earned run early. After the eleventh, we were still tied at one, and though I would have needed to go six more scoreless innings to be ERA leader, I was taken out to avoid injury. Fortunately we scored two in the top of the twelfth, and I got that last elusive win. For the third time in four years, I finished with an even record.

With a record like that it's hard to believe Tony Gwynn and Jack McKeon had such nice things to say about my pitching. But my personal season was legitimately better than the year before because I had only four shutouts and no significant scoreless streak. Though I didn't have 59 scoreless innings at the end of the season, which had lowered my ERA to 2.26 in 1988, I still finished 1989 with an ERA of 2.31, second to Scott Garrelts of the Giants by one earned run. To do that I had to be more consistent. I gave my team a chance to win more of my starts than the year before, and that is my job.

It takes a lot of discipline for a professional athlete to continue to put good numbers on the board in a losing year. It might not show to anyone else if I started sloughing off in my workouts when the team was out of the running. Who but I would know if I ran three-quarter speed or cut my weight training in half? But I wouldn't have been able to look myself in the mirror in the morning. I played a lot of mind games with myself to keep myself disciplined and working hard. I looked for lives to get involved with on our ball club, young players or struggling veterans to encourage.

As frustrating as the outcome of the 1989 season was the reaction of people who think a 15–15 record means I simply fell apart after my 1988 performance. I hate to lose, and there's nowhere I'd rather have been during the post season than in the playoffs and the series. So I'll remain obsessed with the fundamentals, worrying about execution and letting the outcome take care of itself. If you are truly more concerned with the process than the product, then the product won't disappoint you. We did our jobs. We played the best we could. Next year we'll do the same and hope it turns out differently.

You can do exactly what you're supposed to do and still lose. It's not luck; it's the probabilities of baseball. In my own career, what if I had set the scoreless inning record in April of 1988 and had gone flat in September or October? We may not have won the pennant; I may not have been Cy Young award winner. Maybe nothing would have been the same.

This year (1989) was a season to test my theories and my faith. There were those who said it was easy for Orel Hershiser to sing hymns and give credit to God when he was on top of the world, but where is God now? He's still here, and He still loves me, and He is still more important than anything else.

My family is healthy and happy. I have true, dear friends and supportive parents. As spring training nears I'll be in shape, eager for a new season, hoping for additions and changes to the chemistry of the

Dodgers. I'll be ready to work, to give it my all, to compete, to win.

But the only thing that's going to count in the long run is not my won-loss record or how much I wind up with in my bank book. Whether 15–15 or 23–8, in fifty years, no one will remember much about this book or me. But there is one part that could affect you forever. Read chapter nine again. It's the only one that really counts.

APPENDIX

THE NUMBERS

Name:	Hershiser, Orel Leonard IV
Born:	September 16, 1958, Buffalo, New York
Bats:	Right
Throws:	Right
Height:	6 feet 3 inches
Weight:	192
Married:	Jamie Byars, February 7, 1981
Children:	Orel Leonard V (Quinton), November 24, 1984; Jordan Douglas, September 15, 1988
Major League Service:	Six years, 32 days
How Obtained:	Dodger's 17th round selection in Free Agent Draft, June, 1979

CAREER STATISTICS

Regular Season Record

YEAR/CLUB	W–L	ERA	G	GS	CG	SO	SV	IP	H	R	ER	BB	K
1979 Clinton	4–1	2.09	15	4	1	0	2	43.0	3	15	10	17	33
1980 San Antonio	5–9	3.55	49	3	1	0	14	109.0	120	59	43	59	75
1981 San Antonio	7–6	4.68	42	4	3	0	15	102.0	94	54	53	50	95
1982 Albuquerque	9–6	3.70	47	7	2	0	4	132.2	121	73	61	63	93
1983 Albuquerque	10–8	4.09	49	10	6	0	16	134.1	132	73	61	57	95
Los Angeles	0–0	3.38	8	0	0	0	1	8.0	7	6	3	6	5
1984 Los Angeles	11–8	2.66	45	20	8	4	2	189.2	160	65	56	50	150
1985 Los Angeles	19–3	2.03	36	34	9	5	0	239.2	179	72	54	68	157
1986 Los Angeles	14–14	3.85	35	35	8	1	0	234.1	213	112	99	86	153
1987 Los Angeles	16–16	3.06	37	35	10	1	1	264.2	247	105	90	74	190
1988 Los Angeles	23–8	2.26	35	34	15	8	1	267.0	208	73	67	73	178
1989 Los Angeles	15–15	2.31	35	33	8	4	0	256.2	226	75	66	77	178
Maj. Lg. Ttls.	98–64	2.69	231	191	58	23	5	1457.0	1040	508	435	434	1011

League Championship Series Record

YEAR/OPPONENT	W–L	ERA	G	GS	CG	SO	SV	IP	H	R	ER	BB	K
1983 LA vs. Phil	Did not play												
1985 LA vs St.L	1–0	3.52	2	2	1	0	0	15.1	17	6	6	6	5
1988 LA vs NY	1–0	1.46	4	3	1	1	1	24.2	18	5	4	7	15

World Series Record

YEAR/OPPONENT	W–L	ERA	G	GS	CG	SO	SV	IP	H	R	ER	BB	K
1988 LA vs. Oak.	2–0	1.00	2	2	2	1	0	18.0	7	2	2	6	17

1988 STATISTICS

Last Nine Starts

OPPONENT	DATE	W/L	IP	H	R	ER	BB	K
Montreal	8/19	W	9	5	0	0	1	8
New York	8/24	L	9	7	2	2	3	7
Montreal	8/30	W	9	6	2	2	2	9
Atlanta	9/5	W	9	4	0	0	1	8
Cincinnati	9/10	W	9	7	0	0	3	8
Atlanta	9/14	W	9	6	0	0	2	8
Houston	9/19	W	9	4	0	0	0	5
San Francisco	9/23	W	9	5	0	0	2	2
San Diego	9/28	ND	10	4	0	0	1	3

Streak Totals

From the 6th inning of August 30 through the 10th inning of September 26

IP	H	R	ER	BB	K
59	30	0	0	9	34

National League Championship Series

OPPONENT	DATE	W/L	IP	H	R	ER	BB	K
New York	10/5	ND	8.1	7	2	2	1	6
New York	10/8	ND	7	6	3	2	4	4
New York	10/9	S	.1	0	0	0	0	0
New York	10/12	W	9	5	0	0	2	5
Totals		1–0	24.2	18	5	4	7	15

World Series

OPPONENT	DATE	W/L	IP	H	R	ER	BB	K
Oakland	10/16	W	9	3	0	0	2	8
Oakland	10/20	W	9	4	2	2	4	9
Totals		2–0	18	7	2	2	6	17

GLOSSARY

Ace—a team's leading pitcher.

Ahead in the count—for a pitcher, having more strikes than balls on a hitter; for a hitter, the reverse.

Aired out—lectured.

Alley—the gap between left field and center field and between right field and center field.

Away—an outside pitch, as in "low and away."

AWOL—Absent without leave.

Balk—a motion violation by the pitcher. Base runners are allowed to move up one base.

Batting average—number of hits divided by number of at bats (at bats do not include walks, being hit by a pitch, or sacrificing a runner along).

Big club—major league team.

Bloop—a weakly hit ball that falls just beyond the reach of an infielder and an outfielder. See **Texas Leaguer**.

Box—the batter's box.

Complete game—game in which a pitcher both starts and finishes.

Contact hitter—one who seldom strikes out.

Cy Young Award—Title given to the best pitcher in each of the major leagues, named after the winningest pitcher in baseball history.

Designated hitter—American League teams may insert into their lineup a designated hitter in place of any player, usually the pitcher. He bats but does not play in the field.

Dinger—a home run.

Dog days—long stretches of the regular season, usually in the summer months or September.

Double play—when two players are retired on the same play.

Double switch—when a pitcher and a position player are replaced at the same time so the latter can bat in the pitcher's spot and the new pitcher can bat in the other spot in the lineup. This keeps the relief pitcher from hitting sooner than necessary.

Dribbler—see **Squib**.

Earned Run Average (ERA)—The average number of runs a pitcher gives up every nine innings, figured by multiplying the runs by nine and dividing the number of innings pitched.

Earned run—a run earned off the pitcher without the benefit of an error.

Free swinger—a hitter who walks infrequently; swings at anything close.

Hit it out—hit a home run.

Hit-and-run—the runner attempts to steal on the pitch, and the batter attempts to hit behind him to cut down on the chance for a double play.

Junkballer—a pitcher who relies on off-speed pitches.

Knocked out—caused a pitcher to be taken out.

Lay one in—throw a pitch that's easy to hit.

Magic number—the amount of games a team must win or opponents must lose (or a combination of both) to ensure the team will win its division.

No-decision—when a pitcher has appeared in a game and is credited with neither the win nor the loss.

On the bubble—the next to be traded or sent back to the minors.

Opener—first game.

Perfect game—a game in which the opponent does not reach first base, the rarest pitching performance in major league baseball.

Plant—the placement of a pitcher's front foot before he releases the ball.

Pulled-in infield—where the infielders play closer to the plate in an attempt to throw out a runner who would otherwise score on a routine ground ball.

Pumped up—excited. Inspired.

Rag—to jeer or razz.

Relay—throw from a cutoff man or from the middle man in a double play.

Rookie—first-year player.

Sacrifice—when a runner is advanced by the batter bunting into an out or flying out and allowing the runner to score.

Sanitaries—white stockings worn beneath uniform stirrups.

Save—a relief pitching statistic, awarded to the pitcher who protects a lead for the winning pitcher.

Shellacking—see **Shelled.**

Shelled—when a pitcher is hit hard and often.

Shut out—a game in which the opponent does not score.

Skipper—the manager.

Slump—period during which a pitcher doesn't win or a batter hits poorly.

Solo homer—a home run with no runners on base.

Square around—get in position to bunt.

Squib—a poorly hit ball that finds its way between infielders or is hit so slowly that the runner can beat the throw.

Stopper—a starting pitcher known for stopping losing streaks or a relief pitcher known for stopping rallies.

Strength against strength—a pitcher challenging a hitter with his best pitch, even if it's the hitter's favorite type.

Stuff—a pitcher's variety of pitches.

Suicide squeeze—where a runner on third breaks for the plate and the batter bunts the ball. If he misses the pitch, the runner is usually tagged out easily by the catcher.

Sweet spot—an area of the bat where the ball is hit more solidly than any other area.

Taking—when a hitter does not swing.

Texas Leaguer—a batted ball that drops in behind the infield and is too shallow for an outfielder to reach.

The count—the number of strikes and balls on a hitter.

Triple-A—the top level of professional baseball before the majors.

Unearned run—a run produced through no fault of the pitcher, such as via an error, a passed ball, etc.

ABOUT THE WRITER

Jerry B. Jenkins, 39, is Vice President and Writer-in-Residence at the Moody Bible Institute of Chicago. Among his many published works are biographies of Sammy Tippit, Hank Aaron, Dick Motta, Pat Williams, Paul Anderson, Madeline Manning, Walter Payton, B. J. Thomas, Luis Palau, George Sweeting, Meadowlark Lemon, and Christine Wyrtzen.

His adult fiction series (the *Margo Mysteries* and the *Jennifer Grey Mysteries*) have won numerous awards. He has also written *The Operative*, an international espionage thriller. His children's fiction includes the *Baker Street Sports Club*, the *Dallas O'Neil Mysteries*, and the *Bradford Family Adventures*.

Mr. Jenkins is a humorist and frequent writer's conference speaker. He has taught several semesters of graduate school journalism and communications courses. He enjoys international travel.

He and his wife Dianna live with their three children (Dallas, Chad, and Michael) at Three-Son Acres, west of Zion, Illinois. *Out of the Blue* is his 75th book.